D0602665

THE NEW NORTH

THE NEW NORTH

CONTEMPORARY POETRY FROM

NORTHERN IRELAND

EDITED BY CHRIS AGEE

WAKE FOREST UNIVERSITY PRESS

First published in 2008 by Wake Forest University Press
P.O. Box 7333, Winston-Salem, North Carolina 27109-7333

Introduction copyright © 2008 by Chris Agee
Poems and translations copyright © 2008
by authors and translators as acknowledged

All rights reserved. No part of this book may be
reproduced, stored in a retrieval system, or
transmitted in any form, or by any means, electronic,
mechanical, photocopying, recording or otherwise,
without prior written permission from
Wake Forest University Press.

This project is supported in part by an award
from the National Endowment for the Arts.

NATIONAL
ENDOWMENT
FOR THE ARTS
A great nation
deserves great art.

Cover image: *To Be With*, copyright © Sean Scully,
1996, 108 × 180 inches. Collection of Museum
Moderner Kunst Stiftung Ludwig, Vienna, Austria.
Used with kind permission of the artist.
Designed and composed by Quemadura
Printed on acid-free, recycled paper in
the United States by Thomson-Shore

ISBN 978-1-930630-35-2
LCCN 2008930375

All true creators of language know that they are creating life
as they write. The life of language, the life of the language.

NUALA NÍ DHOMHNAILL

CONTENTS

CLASSIC POEMS

MATT KIRKHAM

GEARÓID MAC LOCHLAINN

ALAN GILLIS

PREFACE

The New North: Contemporary Poetry from Northern Ireland was edited by an American-born poet, Chris Agee, who has made his life and forged his career in Northern Ireland. Mr Agee has been in a special position to view poetic life here from both an internal and external perspective. The Arts Council of Northern Ireland would like to thank him for undertaking the selection of poetry for this anthology. Special thanks are also due to the publisher of *The New North*, Wake Forest University Press in Winston-Salem, North Carolina. Press Director Jefferson Holdridge and Assistant Director Candide Jones worked attentively with Mr Agee to produce this handsome publication.

The quality and breadth of the poetry that you will experience in this anthology need no further introduction than that provided by the editor. For the opportunity to present it to the American public, however, the Arts Council of Northern Ireland gratefully acknowledges and recognises the energetic leadership of Dana Gioia, Chairman of the National Endowment for the Arts, in the conception of the international literary exchange which brought about both *The New North* and *New Voices: Contemporary Poetry from the United States*, the counterpart volume to be published in Northern Ireland by the Belfast-based publisher, Irish Pages. We also much appreciate the oversight of the whole project generously undertaken by Jon Peede, Director for Literature, and Pennie Ojeda, Director for International Activities, both of the National Endowment for the Arts.

The context in which this project was created is linked to Northern Ireland's participation in the forty-first presentation of the Smithsonian Institution's extraordinary Folklife Festival in Washington, DC during the summer of 2007. No one could have envisaged the far-reaching effects our presence there would have. It was a unique opportunity to present a new image of Northern Ireland in the very heart of the United States, an updated profile of how far our people had travelled during a period of almost ten years of peace.

Few in the rest of the world had realised the immensity of the changes in our society. Few were aware of the new cohesion of our political environment. Few had experienced the new healing of our community divisions.

Our aim in the Folklife Festival was to present the rich historical foundations of our current vibrant culture. To complement this two-week cultural feast, Northern Ireland also embarked upon a four-month lead-up series of events in Washington, DC. This Rediscover Northern Ireland programme reflected the wider artistic life of our society. At its heart were the artists, the actors, the musicians, the writers and the poets. Out of all proportion to the small size of our population, these were the people who promoted creativity, inspired imaginations and offered visionary sustenance in a sometimes embattled and often stark reality.

Amongst the many partners in Washington, DC who came to our help with generous and practical offers of support in seeding the sixty-six arts events of Rediscover Northern Ireland was the National Endowment for the Arts. The Arts Council of Northern Ireland was and remains profoundly grateful for this collegial alliance which in April 2007 blossomed into an evening of poetry at the National Geographic Society. It featured on stage three poets from Northern Ireland who are renowned international doyens in the world of poetry, Michael Longley, Ciaran Carson and Paul Muldoon—with an exclusive filmed interview and reading by Seamus Heaney. Appropriately, the event was introduced by the poet and Chairman of the National Endowment for the Arts, Dana Gioia. It was an evening which I, and no doubt many others, will never forget.

As a result of that event, and out of the creative friendship that grew between the institutions of the National Endowment for the Arts and the Arts Council of Northern Ireland, two new anthologies of poetry have been compiled to reflect the work of new generations of poets presently emerging in the United States and in Northern Ireland.

—DR PHILIP HAMMOND
Creative Director of Rediscover Northern Ireland

INTRODUCTION

I

The island of Ireland lies at the western extremity of the Eurasian landmass, straddling the same circumpolar latitudes as Newfoundland, with only the Atlantic between its westernmost counties and the next parish in America. It is about the size of West Virginia, and its population, now numbering well over five million, is approximately that of Tennessee. Despite its northerliness, the island possesses the clement and temperate climate meteorologists call 'oceanic', warmed by the Gulf Stream swinging up past New England and the Maritimes, and swept by an endless procession of Atlantic weathers, often of dazzling changeability.

In 1920, during the War of Independence, which pitted Irish republican secessionists against the constitutional order of British rule, Ireland—previously a single polity—was partitioned into two jurisdictions. Partition was the culmination of the armed insurrection launched by a self-formed militia, the Irish Volunteers, on Easter Monday, 1916, during which an Irish republic was proclaimed; in his monumental poem 'Easter, 1916', William Butler Yeats memorialises the meaning of the violent genesis of Irish independence for those, like himself, whose aspirations had long lain in this direction.

With the end of the War of Independence, all twenty-three southern and western counties in the provinces of Leinster, Munster, and Connaught, as well as three northern counties in Ulster, formed a new independent Irish 'Free State', which subsequently ended its British dominion status and formally declared itself a Republic, with a written constitution, in 1949. This unseasonable division was sealed by the disposition of political, cultural, and military considerations when the Treaty ending the hostilities was agreed in 1921 by republican leaders and the British Government.

Upon the signing of the Treaty, however, Irish republicanism split over its terms, and for the next year a bitter civil war ensued in Southern Ireland between the supporters and opponents of the Treaty's acceptance of Partition. Yeats was again imaginatively at hand: in 'Nineteen Hundred and Nineteen' and 'Meditations in Time of Civil War', he records the doubts and cruelties attendant on the violence, as it bled first into atrocity, and thence to the internecine horrors of the Civil War.

Meanwhile about a sixth of the island, the six remaining Ulster counties in the northeast, about the size of Connecticut, stayed with Britain and, in 1922, were constitutionally christened 'Northern Ireland', with its own Parliament and Prime Minster under the devolved authority of the Westminster Parliament in London. What had been the *United Kingdom of Great Britain and Ireland*, formed from two distinct Kingdoms by the Act of Union in 1801 and covering all of 'the British Isles', had now shrunk to that Union's remnant, the renamed *United Kingdom of Great Britain and Northern Ireland*. As the full name makes plain, Northern Ireland is not, and has never been, formally a part of Great Britain—itself the product of an Act of Union between the Kingdoms of England and Scotland, in 1707—even if the sobriquet 'Britain' is still used loosely to describe this longstanding multinational state under a single monarchy.

Behind the Partition of Ireland lay a deeper cultural pattern that was integral to the constitutional outcome. It is easy to overstate the historic distinctiveness of Ulster within the island's interrelated cultural geography when compared to the neighbouring island; but that such Ulster distinctiveness has existed and still does, in many essential ways, is vouchsafed by a voluminous historiography dealing with the province over many centuries.

Much of Irish history hinges on the island's relations with its larger, more powerful, and expansionist neighbour to the east. By the beginning of the early modern period—the Tudor period in England—Ireland was already characterized by a linguistic, cultural and political divide that would frame its subsequent history. In the 'English Pale' around Dublin, and in domains of the Anglo-Norman magnates whose families had been settled for centuries in eastern and south-eastern Ireland, the English Crown held feudal sway, at least nominally, having assumed 'the lordship of Ireland' in the twelfth century; but the greater part of the country was divided into a large number of regions, up to fifty or sixty, each of which was virtually an independent state, ruled over by a native chief or by a Anglo-Norman noble. In the remoter regions of the west and north especially, 'the native Irish' persisted unchallenged, and the loose congeries of tribal kingdoms that constituted an indigenous Gaelic order of great antiquity—pastoral and aristocratic in spirit, with its own system of law and revered body of oral and written learning—remained largely intact through the Tudor period.

Towards the end of sixteenth century, Ulster had become the prime obstacle to the extension of royal power, and the associated process of Anglicisation in law and culture, across the whole of Ireland. There, behind a formidable barrier of lake and mountain, the Gaelic order held a last fastness. Faced with a rebellion led by Hugh O'Neill in defence of Gaelic separatism, Queen Elizabeth launched a series of military campaigns aimed at the final conquest of Ulster. Lytton Strachey's famous account of the failure of Essex's Irish campaign, and subsequent execution, tells the tale from the perspective of the English Court. By 1607, after the failed intervention of Catholic Spain at Kinsale, the Tudor conquest was complete, Gaelic independence broken, and the two most prominent native Ulster earls in flight to the Continent.

In the succeeding decades, the English government initiated a policy of settling, or 'planting', English and lowland Scots colonists in Ulster on the confiscated lands of the Gaelic nobles, in order to secure permanently the writ of royal power. Thus began 'the Plantation of Ulster' lasting, in one form or another, for the rest of the seventeenth century. The native Catholic Irish of all classes in Ulster were progressively disenfranchised and marginalized. Though the plantation policy was extended outside of Ulster, it was much less successful elsewhere in Ireland.

Ulster's Plantation was further intensified by the Cromwellian conquest and settlement across much of the island in the mid-seventeenth century, and culminated with new waves of Protestant Williamite settlers after William of Orange's defeat of James II and his assumption of the English throne, following what was, in effect, a pan-European conflict between Protestant and Catholic superpowers of the day, fought partly in Ireland. In England, the triumph of William in 1688 became known as 'the Glorious Revolution'; in Ireland, it represented the final triumph of a minority 'Protestant ascendancy'—in land ownership, governance, and religion—whose rule would be entrenched by a series of draconian anti-Catholic penal laws in force until the last decades of the eighteenth century.

The Plantation of Ulster was, then, foundational in its influence over the subsequent history of the province. It is the historical *longue durée* both of the particular Irish distinctiveness of Ulster and the eventual political Partition of the island. Of course, the influence of the Plantation progressively decanted, evolved, morphed, modulated, and even flowered under innumerable guises—the empirical stuff of history—over the succeeding three centuries. But few familiar with the North of Ireland would gainsay that it also endowed the geography in question with an abiding, if always fluid, history of cultural bifurcation, a kind of psychic partition on common ground, or within much-shared ways-of-life—between the perspectives of the Planter and the Gael, the Protestant and the Catholic, the unionist and the nationalist, or some mix or foreswearing thereof—the extraordinary tenacity of which is historically striking.

At certain periods, such as the 1790s or early 1960s, the antagonisms attendant on this antique Ulster pluralism have waned markedly, as pursuit of common objectives took hold; at others, such as the aftermath of Partition or during the Troubles, they waxed into civil tumult and bloodshed. So, emblematically, in a number of early poems and essays, we find Seamus Heaney using—or dwelling on—the compound place-name 'Mossbawn' (*bawn*, from the Irish *bábhún*: a fortified enclosure built by Plantation settlers), precisely to bring to light a prospect of mind tuned to this complex Ulster dynamic, whereby the vicinity of his rural upbringing was simultaneously a 'country of community' and a 'realm of division'.

The dynamic of Partition was, then, never a simple function of the insular histories of the two islands. If the emergence of Northern Ireland was the long-distance descendant of the Plantation, it can also be understood as the terminus to a great swathe of lands shaped by the Reformation, arcing from Central and Northern Europe, into the British-and-Irish archipelago. Likewise, the cognate independence of the South belongs to a much later pan-European cultural pattern; namely, the small nations of Europe, the so-called Succession States, that emerged out of the imperial aftermath of the First World War. These dozen states created from the successor territories of four empires (Russian, Austro-Hungarian, British, Ottoman) were formed at the same period (1918-1921) and under the influence of much the same nationalist and republican ideals; but with the exception of Ireland, they all belonged to Eastern or Central Europe and the Balkans. Subsequently, the Baltic States were ingested by the Soviet Union and the very recollection of the *Mitteleuropa* of the interwar period was obscured by the Cold War division of Europe.

In this European perspective, the creation of Northern Ireland eighty-six years ago was, willy-nilly, the product of the very same ascendant continental pattern that brought into existence the Succession States. Even if the North was not itself, properly speaking, one of those states, remaining a loyal remnant of an older multinational Union, it was nonetheless a new constitutional European jurisdiction and, in this sense, one of the new small succession 'countries' of post-Versailles Europe — being about the size of Flanders, in Belgium.

In the interwar period, reconfigured Europe abounded in nationally-ambiguous territories, recent annexations and re-unifications, condominiums or Free Cities of divided loyalties that largely vanished into the unchallenged consolidation of borders after the Second World War. In contrast, having been shielded by Britain from the ravages of total war, what Winston Churchill called 'the integrity of their quarrel' apropos the two Northern Irish traditions was set to persist far into the post-war period. If such dynamics are amenable to grand theories, it might be said that Northern Ireland had emerged out of the historical equivalent of two colliding tectonic plates, one foundational, one contemporary: the Reformation in Ireland, and the disintegration of internal European empires.

11

After Partition, relations between the two parts of Ireland entered a political and cultural deep-freeze. Partition territorialized, and therefore intensified and fossilized, the very tectonic forces that engendered it, which had been more diffuse, complex and variegated across the previous single Irish polity. Two religio-political monoliths—Catholic-nationalist, Protestant-unionist—held ideological sway, largely unchallenged, across their respective states for the first half-century of constitutional division.

In both parts of Ireland, it was widely felt that the new southern State was more insular and isolationist, less developed in the modern sense, compared to its Northern neighbour. The Free State emerged into independence as a mainly agrarian society faced with the post-imperial challenges of nation-building and depleted by emigration. During the Second World War, it declared 'The Emergency' and remained neutral; not until the late 1950s was a full-scale policy of industrialization initiated, which lay the basis for the much-increased prosperity of the next decade. Irish literary writing from the forties to the seventies—from Patrick Kavanagh's long poem 'The Great Hunger' (1942) on the privations of rural life, to Anthony Cronin's Dublin memoir, *Dead as Doornails* (1976)—is replete with a sense of generalized stagnation having overcome the promise of the new State.

Yet from the establishment of the Republic onwards, the South was essentially a normalized European state, albeit one of an intensely conservative and Catholic temper. Slowly, it shed some of the more conflicted intensities of its post-imperial legacy. Owing partly to the prominence of nationalist Protestant writers in the independence movement, such as W.B. Yeats and Douglas Hyde (the first President of Ireland), the southern State never instituted a systemic policy of discrimination against its minority community, despite the undoubted informal reach of religious prejudice. In the mid-fifties, the German novelist and later Nobel Laureate, Heinrich Böll, began spending time in the West of Ireland; and his marvellous account of that period, *Irish Journal* (1957), evokes the fundamental positive of independence, however impoverished; reminding us that 'eighteen months before Lenin took over the remains of an empire, the Irish poets were scraping away the first stone from under the pedestal of that other empire which was regarded as indestructible but has since turned out to be far from it'.

Up North, the first half-century of Partition took on a very different complexion. As with the reciprocal image of the South, it was widely perceived across the island that the North was more prosperous and socially progressive than its independent neighbour. The country had inherited a large nineteenth- and early twentieth-century industrial base, and the great achievements of the British welfare state, such as the National Health Service and the post-war Education Acts, covered the whole of the United Kingdom. Belfast in particular was the island's gate to the wider, wealthier world of Britain and its still far-flung empire.

From the start, though, comparative prosperity and British social advance were darkened by egregious inequities in the local body politic. For the whole of its existence until 1972, Northern Ireland was a one-party unionist state of highly authoritarian hue, ruled with large measures of sectarian callousness, religio-ethnic superiority, and middle-class complacency.

The position of the bulk of the Catholic population—especially the urban working classes—verged continually on the dire. Gerrymandering, housing and employment discrimination, forced emigration, and a sectarian police force were cumulatively designed to thwart any possibility of minority political challenge—whether from the viewpoint of constitutional nationalism, or of traditional militant republicanism—to the Union and unionist rule. The prevailing status of Catholics as second-class citizens was similar in tone—if not in degree—to the Jim Crow régime in the American South. Apologists for pre-Troubles Northern Ireland often speak of the unifying communal decencies of the middle ground and the great charms and attributes of the country, and these of course existed in abundance; but for the full picture, one need only turn to Heaney's poem, 'The Ministry of Fear', to glimpse how ominous things felt from inside the minority community in the 1950s.

By the mid-sixties, Northern Ireland was beginning to liberalize. Inspired by the civil rights movement in America, a Civil Rights Association was formed and initiated a campaign of consciousness-raising and civil protest on behalf of equal rights for Catholics, who comprised about 40% of the population. Significantly, it not only garnered mass street support from the minority community, but a considerable degree of encouragement from liberal Protestant opinion. The movement's early momentum was, however, stymied by a fierce, and sometimes violent, counter-reaction by the unionist government and its essentially hard-line political base, or militant loyalist and Orange Order allies. The stage was set for a full-blown civil eruption.

It came in August 1969. The spark was widespread house-burning by loyalist mobs, with some connivance by the police, in Catholic districts of Belfast, following nationalist riots in Derry; but Partition's accumulation of minority grievance and unionist intransigence, the worldwide insurrectional atmosphere of the late sixties, republican idealism, the self-perpetuating nature of sectarian communal violence, and a host of other factors— the stuff, again, of empirical history—now all combined to launch 'the Troubles'.

Within days, the British Government dispatched troops from 'the mainland' to protect Catholic districts and stabilize the situation. Successive waves of escalating events fed into the descending vortex of crisis. With hindsight, it is striking that it took two years, until 1971, for both republican and loyalist paramilitaries to emerge centre-stage. In August 1971 'internment without trial' was introduced, aimed mainly at a resurgent IRA and other republicans. In January 1972, British paratroopers shot dead thirteen unarmed protesters in Derry—at a stroke radicalising the Catholic community, and further buoying recruitment by the IRA. Shortly afterwards, the British Government prorogued the Parliament of Northern Ireland and instituted 'direct rule' from the Cabinet in London, through the Northern Irish civil service—a 'provisional' constitutional arrangement that would last another three decades. When the IRA exploded twenty-two bombs in Belfast on a single day in July 1972, killing nine people and wounding over a hundred, the Troubles had reached a new nadir of violent mayhem that threatened to spin completely out of control.

To speak, however, of *war* in the context of the Troubles is highly prob-
lematic. Apart from the formal military legitimacy it confers on paramilitary
formations, the word lacks empirical verification. The classic definition of
war is open and organized military conflict between states, in situations of
occupation as defined by the Geneva Conventions, or in zones of indis-
putable colonialism unmediated by democracy and the post-war under-
standing of human rights. In a basic anthropological sense, war is the reign
of violence, the complete suspension of civil society—and that, apart from
certain inklings in the seventies, was never approached in Northern Ireland.
The Northern writer always addressed a large and functioning civil society
in the North, not to mention those of Britain and the Republic. There have
been civil violence, insurrection, bloodlust, ethnic clearances, terrorism,
counter-terrorism, and so forth—but never the full anthropological activity
evident in Homer, Wilfred Owen, or Primo Levi.

In 1974, the British Government brokered the Sunningdale Agreement,
which envisaged permanent power-sharing between unionism and national-
ism in a devolved government for Northern Ireland, but it was quickly un-
done by a generalized Protestant revolt led by paramilitaries, the Ulster Work-
ers Council Strike, perhaps the largest popular uprising in post-war Western
Europe. Thenceforward, the search was on for a constitutional solution that
would bring the Troubles to an end. It was to take, alas, a full quarter-century.

With unionist rule abandoned and the British government committed to
holding the ring with shaky even-handedness, *faute de mieux*—though it
hardly worked out that way—it was as if the Troubles had hunkered down
into a steady-state equilibrium between mostly irreconcilable forces. A large
peace movement arose, then waned in face of the intractable dynamic. Nor-
mal life went on, often little-troubled directly by the political situation, es-
pecially in more prosperous urban areas, many of the small towns, and large
swathes of the countryside—even if the oppressive and funereal atmosphere
of the Troubles hung heavy everywhere in the North.

Essential stalemate was shadowed by the infamous milestones it gener-
ated: the Hunger Strikes by republican prisoners; the Brighton bombing, just

missing much of the British Cabinet; an interminable litany of political and sectarian murder and maiming. And so on—and on. This was the long period in which political stasis, cyclical violence, and generalized social and economic stagnation became second nature to a riven culture. Each of the contributors to *The New North*—as child, youth, and/or young adult – would have lived though this marathon prospect, and known it intimately, for various periods of time, and from whatever vantage point their life-narratives brought to bear.

Then, in the late eighties and early nineties, a series of initiatives was embarked upon jointly by the British and Irish governments that led to some movement in the glacial equilibrium. In August 1994, the IRA, recognizing the cul-de-sac nature of the stalemate, declared a cessation of hostilities against the British state. Michael Longley's brief poem, 'Ceasefire' (p. 16), published the next week in *The Irish Times*, captured for many the intense but ambiguous emotions of that moment. Seldom can a poem have had such instant public meaning.

A 'peace process' soon got under way under the aegis of the two governments. After four arduous years of negotiation, all but one of the main political parties signed up to 'The Belfast Agreement', a new constitutional dispensation for devolved government in Northern Ireland, based on power-sharing between the two communities, and hedged round with clauses recognizing their permanent parity in all matters of law, social policy, and culture. On the day the Agreement was finally signed, after a final bout of all-night negotiations—Good Friday morning, 1998—euphoria swept Ireland.

The North would remain part of the United Kingdom, but the Republic would have a recognized constitutional role in a series of specified areas. Significantly, the Agreement was approved by referenda in both parts of Ireland, and incorporated in the constitutional law of Britain and the Republic. The document was a masterpiece of astute, deft, and at points ambiguous phraseology. This is partly the reason, over the next decade, that implementation of the Agreement proceeded at a snail's pace, with the first devolved government foundering on continuing political disputes and leading to a reinstatement of direct rule for several years. Finally, the last logjam of issues was overcome, with a supplementary agreement, and in May 2007, all four main parties entered a new devolved government as a single Grand Coalition.

For the first time since the formation of Northern Ireland, the state had the explicit support of the large majority of both communities. But what exactly was this state? For the polity that exited the Troubles was profoundly different from the vanished unionist bastion of four decades earlier.

Is it a permanent remnant of an older Union, the lost province of a future unified Irish nation, or one of the small countries of Europe? In according various degrees of formal legitimacy to each of these perspectives, the Agreement consciously foreclosed on the possibility of a single constitutional answer. 'All' or 'none' might easily be construed as more plausible answers. For instance, in terms of culture and geography, rather than law and economy, the North does not really or fully belong to the British state, despite the titular jurisdiction, a truth underscored for Great Britain by the Troubles themselves; at the same time, it has become quite distant in many important cultural and social respects from the Republic.

The natural tendency of any polity to bolster the autonomy of its own civic life is, however, well under way. In the current period of dramatic cultural and economic transformation following The Belfast Agreement, Northern Ireland (current population: 1.7 million) can often seem akin to a 'city state'—Belfast, and all its hinterland within easy driving distance—or even a kind of 'anti-state', where classic sovereignty has been diluted in the name of the native ground, or common good.

III

This anthology brings together 15 poets born between 1956 and 1975. With one exception, these poets have published their collections in the two decades before and after the Belfast Agreement. In this sense, they represent the first clear poetic grouping—or, loosely, 'publishing generation'—since the two previous celebrated generations of Northern Irish poets (born between 1939 and 1952) that emerged in the 1960s and 1970s. Just as the appearance of those earlier generations spanned the last decade of the old North and the first decade of the Troubles, so this grouping straddles the last years of the Troubles and the first of the new North.

Apart from the poetry itself (published in one collection at least), I assembled the anthology on the basis of three criteria. Each of the contributors had to satisfy one of the following: 1) born, raised and resident in Northern Ireland; 2) born, raised but no longer resident in Northern Ireland; 3) neither born nor raised in Northern Ireland, but resident there for a substantial period, with a clear presence in the Northern literary scene and/or published work informed, in whatever way, by life in the North.

In order to avoid the ethnic essentialism that so often attaches to 'Irish poet', it was highly important to get these categories right; for, in the same way, it would be invidious to distinguish between British or American writers who are 'native-born' and those who are citizens by virtue of naturalisation or residence (e.g., Salman Rushdie or Charles Simic). Thus the subtitle to this anthology refers not to 'poets', but to the slightly more expansive, and precise, 'poetry'.

The need for such careful criteria is strengthened by the ambiguous constitutional identity of Northern Ireland itself. Notwithstanding the ethnic fixity suggested by the Troubles, Northern Ireland has, in fact, always been something of a 'cultural corridor' (Edna Longley) since Partition, with significant resident populations from Scotland, England and the Republic, in addition to large-scale immigration, both old and new, mainly from Hong Kong, the Subcontinent, Poland, the Baltics and Africa—none of which can be ignored in any consideration of the actually-existing culture. Moreover, owing to its Constitution, the Republic will grant passports, on application, to most of those born in Northern Ireland; in other words, a very high proportion of the North's indigenous population have opted *not* to apply for British citizenship and, consequently, often hold passports issued by another state. Under the Belfast Agreement, the population is further promised dual citizenship in perpetuity. By a strange irony, the North is inescapably multinational and, increasingly, multicultural.

Without any prior intention, this complex if less obvious cultural pattern is reflected by The New North. Regarding the three criteria, ten poets belong to the first category, two to the second, and four to the third (of which one is from the Republic, one from Scotland, one from England, and one from the United States). So it is truly an anthology symbolic of the new North — a North of old and new immigration, diaspora, bilingualism, and cultural interchange between the islands, all under the aegis of a new political dispensation that is rapidly weakening the old certainties enforced by the Troubles, towards a destination as yet undetermined.

Two of the poets write in Irish. Gaelic (as it was called historically) is, of course, the old language of Ulster; and whilst it has always been spoken in Northern Ireland, it has also undergone an important revival over the past few decades, especially in Belfast. This survival-into-revival makes it apposite that the work of Cathal Ó Searcaigh stands at the beginning of The New North. A native-speaker from Donegal, his blás, or accent, belongs to the same distinct dialect spoken across the North. As one of the major Irish-language writers, he has been a vital presence for Irish-speakers in the province, including Gearóid Mac Lochlainn, the first important poet to emerge from the contemporary Belfast Gaeltacht.

All anthologies involve choices and cut-offs. My commissioned brief to limit The New North to poets born after 1955 has meant that a number of fine older poets who published later in life could not be accommodated. If by age they belong to the two earlier generations of Northern Irish poets, their publishing histories fall within the last decade or so. Their work awaits some future anthology.

'Reading well,' the English poet and critic Al Alvarez reminds us, 'means opening your ears to the presence behind the words and knowing which notes are true and which are false. It is as much an art as writing well and almost as hard to acquire.' Part of the art of reading poetry lies, then, in a negative capability, the active perception of the false note—an alertness to the techniques, tones, formulae, imitations, postures, fashions, and so forth that might be judged to mar 'the presence behind the words'.

In making my final choice of poets, I have eschewed any body of work characterized by the vatic, the euphonious, the manneristic, the now-conventional poesy of sensuous descriptiveness, the ill-hewn surreal—tendencies that are perhaps characteristic vices in Northern poetry. Nor have I been much attracted to what Harry Clifton has called the poetic 'nostalgia for some lost Northern Irish mind-moment'; and the cognate over-self-consciousness about 'the well-crafted Northern lyric', or any self-interested, self-mythologizing use of 'the Northern thing' that risks an update of 'the Celtic fringe'. Equally, I took it for granted that, poetically speaking, the apparent 'smaller thing', true to its scale, will prove more artistically enduring than the ostensible 'larger thing', failed by the false note.

Certain chameleon styles seemed to substitute a simulacrum of inherited tones for the distinctiveness of true originality, and to exemplify the truth of the American poet Stanley Kunitz's dictum about craft: 'A badly made thing falls apart. It takes only a few years for most of the energy to leak out of a defective work of art. To put it simply, conservation of energy is the function of form.' In short, any perceived omission from the anthology is likely to reflect my sense of what Wallace Stevens called art's requisite 'accuracy with respect to the structure of reality', on top of which all other claims of style and sensibility must be built.

An important dimension of *The New North* are the two sections entitled 'Classic Poems'. These assemble three poems for each of the six poets most identified with the two earlier celebrated poetic generations. Behind this novel feature of the anthology lies an approach to generational influence. The current situation has parallels with the shadow of achievement thrown by Yeats during the first poetic generations of the new Irish state; and the classic poems—touchstones for the signature brilliance of each style—are meant to convey some sense of the tradition preceding the work assembled here.

In this way, the previous two generations might be glimpsed briefly in the round, and so allow for firsthand comparisons, within the anthology itself, between the major predecessors and the poets of *The New North*. The classic poems allow the reader to glimpse some fascinating poetic decantings, descents and cross-currents of influence and reaction. Probably such a compact snapshot of the evolution of a poetic tradition is only available to a small culture or nation—hence one of the anthology's especial characteristics, in contradistinction to the larger and more amorphous literary world of the United States, or those of other powerful 'metropolitan' nations.

I V

It might be said of Ireland, as of many small European nations with an ancient pedigree: *small size, big space*. Although the actual territory is constricted, the cultural and historical 'space' is rich, various and dense in a way that, say, the largely natural and unsettled spaces of Wyoming would not be. It is thus one of the unique glories of the Irish cultural 'space' that, over the past century, it has made such an enormous contribution to poetry in particular and world literature in general—including, of course, the efflorescence of Northern poetry that has dominated recent critical perception of the art in Ireland.

If Belfast has seen 'the most important flowering of poetry in the Anglophone world of the last fifty years' (Edward Larrissy), how exactly did this emerge from such a small place, previously to some degree a literary backwater, particularly if one excludes the earlier émigré poets, Louis MacNeice, W. R. Rogers, John Hewitt, Robert Greacen and John Montague? Just the happenstance intersection of talent and territory? For not one, but two poetic generations?

Somehow this seems insufficient as a *full* explanation. For talent obviously emerges from, and is shaped by, the background territory: each significant poet, writes Helen Vendler, 'preserves some part of the culture that would lapse unrecorded were it not for art'. Adrian Frazier has well-described the cultural and critical puzzle: 'The literary achievements of a small number of citizens of this little island in the twentieth century is one of the magnificent mysteries in the history of human culture. We still don't know how it came to pass or have the measure of its magnificence.' The same might be—indeed, often has been—said of the sudden acceleration of painting in the Florentine city state during the Renaissance.

Clearly the efflorescence of major poetry in the North since the sixties can be seen as a subset of Frazier's comment. And just as the Northern Troubles can be understood partly as a follow-on to the troubled Civil War period in the South, so Northern poetry of recent decades has parallels with the cultural revitalizations of the Irish Literary Revival early in the century. But from what direction came the vitalizing context *common* to these individual talents? Surely Florence itself had something to do with the talents of Florentine painting?

Neither literary essentialism ('the Northern poem') nor the predominance of particular styles and cultural tones seems a convincing avenue of explanation—so the tack must go elsewhere. What if Occam's razor was applied and the obvious cultural context, the city-state smallness of the North itself—and the related compactness of its recent poetic 'tradition', in the sense of the intense and challenging mutual self-awareness of practitioners —was carefully attended to?

Small cultures possess particular strengths and energies that are often invisible and largely unavailable (or at least not so easily available) to the bigger psycho-spatial territories of classic 'metropolitan' cultures. 'Metropolitan' perspectives always tend to assume that the larger culture must subsume the strengths of the smaller 'peripheral' one, apart from local colour, whilst possessing many more of its own; but this is hardly the case, as the disproportionate achievements of Northern Irish poetry rather dramatically exemplify in the contemporary British context.

Trying to explain the crystalline clarity of art and letters in classical Greece, the Irish essayist Hubert Butler once remarked: 'The constant friction and fusion of diverse personalities in a confined space caused some creative combustion and sparked off explosions of genius, which could not have happened in those large loose federations, which the Greeks despised.' Something akin, I think, has occurred with poetry in the confined cultural space of the North. The image of 'creative combustion', involving friction as well as fusion, seems close to the literary actuality.

First books by Seamus Heaney (1966), Derek Mahon (1969) and Michael Longley (1969) appeared before the outbreak of the Troubles. Hot on their heels, the débuts of a second generation followed: Paul Muldoon (1973), Ciaran Carson (1976), Frank Ormsby (1977), Tom Paulin (1977) and Medbh McGuckian (1980). Longley, Mahon and Heaney all knew each other from an early stage. Prior to their first collections, Longley and Heaney attended 'The Group', a loose gathering of young writers in Belfast—organized by the poet and academic Philip Hobsbaum of Queen's University Belfast—who met for sessions of practical criticism, discussion, friendship and controversy. All these poets have lived in Belfast for varying periods—four for most of their lives—and all would know the rest well, both as artists and personalities. During these two decades, the city itself was undoubtedly the prime creative locus for their interactions. Varieties of energy—personal, generational, cultural, formal, intellectual, ancestral—combusted into 'explosions of genius'.

That Heaney, Longley and Mahon had by the outbreak of the Troubles already 'found an uninhabited place in the zodiac of poetry' (Vendler) seems quite significant in retrospect. They had apprenticed to the craft and printed their sign in the firmament well before the intense challenge to consciousness posed by violence. The early sixties were heady days for contemporary poetry in Britain especially; and the rich influences of Ted Hughes, Philip Larkin, Hugh MacDiarmid, Dylan Thomas and Geoffrey Hill had been absorbed by the three poets, mingling with many more from the poetries of Ireland, America and contemporary Europe. In their accounts, it is clear that an old dynamic, the friendship of young poets, was a key component in this generational élan. Aerobic intensities fed into each other. One senses a density of encounter, influence and challenge: a cross-hatching of the creative and personal.

When the Troubles hit, all these poets had to rise to the occasion and find 'images and symbols adequate to our predicament' (Heaney). Although first books by the next generation appeared after the start of the Troubles, this new generation too had come to adulthood in more peaceable times. Both poetic generations were united by a common historical predicament. Their poetic ways and means were highly various, but holding one's breath in the changed atmosphere was not an option.

Energies of creative interaction were ramped up in the context of a damaged, and damaging, society. The poets of both generations might be likened to long-distance runners from Africa whose prowess is engendered by the demands of their high-altitude climes. Much has been said about the influence of the Troubles on their work and international standing; it is perhaps best to view the debt in terms of imagination's aerobic training, partly precipitated by the historical moment, but to be deployed on the world at large. After all, Dante wrote universally at a time when Florence was racked by narrow internecine strife.

As Michael Longley has remarked, no poem is a solo flight; peers were listening to each other; and 'to be a poet is to be alive to both precursors and contemporaries'. Such close listening is likely to be at a lesser pitch in more normal societies. The sense of quasi-autarky that descended on the North during the Troubles may also have made its poets more immune to the suasions of those fashionable tones and modes that are always sweeping lightly through the Anglophone poetry world. Absorption of stylistic and imaginative influences—inherently far-flung and individual—had to be flight-tested against a cultural clime instinct with history's exigencies.

There is a further sense of unlocked energies entering poetry: those of the North itself. The collapsed mantle of unionist rule released a hidden Ulster in many artistic directions. Much of Ulster's cultural 'bifurcation' had been kept under tabs, even to itself, by the post-imperial atmosphere of a domineering Britishness. What has often been noticed about Heaney—'it is as though the particulars of life on an Ulster farm were inventing a language for themselves—a dialect that our senses seem always to have known' (Longley)—might be extended in equivalent ways to the five other poets represented in 'Classic Poems'. Each coalesced language and vision into the combination of new attitude, new territory and new accuracy that distinguishes original poetry.

In Western Europe during the same period, no other group of poets experienced anything approximating the ferocity of the Troubles. As in certain poetries in Eastern Europe, historical consciousness had collided with the lyric, occasioning a final energy of interaction with Yeats's example at a prefigurative moment in the history of Ireland. His poetry proved exemplary for its moments of consciousness of the terrible pressure of history concentrated into powerful metaphor.

V

A great deal began to be written about these two generations, most of which focussed on Seamus Heaney. By the mid-eighties, the future Nobel Laureate was well on his way to becoming the most celebrated poet in the Anglophone world. In his extraordinary wake, the critical perception of 'Ulster poetry' went global. Northern Ireland came to loom large on the map of world poetry.

But who would be in the third generation of Northern poets? It was a natural question in a small culture where the field is limited; and amongst those concerned, there soon developed some expectation of a quick poetic succession. It was obvious that whichever poets were so recognized would benefit from the existing enormous interest in Northern Irish poetry. In a fascinating piece of literary sociology, this trope of a third Ulster poetic succession had particular resonance within the university, critical and publishing worlds. Just as generals tend to fight the last war, so there was an unreflective presumption that any new poetic grouping would follow the pattern of the two earlier generations.

As the North's oldest and largest university, Queen's University Belfast became the local portal of this worldwide interest in Ulster poetry. Its close association with many Irish and British poets in recent decades has been a well-justified source of institutional pride. Much distinguished scholarship on Northern Irish poetry has emerged from its School of English.

Still, the presumption that Queen's would always be the epicentre of poetry in the North soon became a limiting paradigm. Aspirant poets continued to join the longstanding Queen's University Writers Group, with the glory days of 'The Group' never far from anyone's mind. In certain critical quarters, there was a concern to manage the Ulster brand, to king-make in Lilliput, and to parlay reputations into the British literary world. The university itself now uses 'Poetry at Queen's' as a marketing slogan. Whilst it cannot be doubted that Queen's will always be central to the North's small poetry world, it is debatable whether this inertial yet emphatic identification of the university with Northern poetry is an authentic perspective. New poetic energies cannot be programmed by such bounded expectations.

Publishing histories are telling in every literary culture. They are particularly so in Northern Ireland, owing to its constitutional ambiguity and its related lack of any dedicated poetry-publishing until the mid-nineties. Previously, it was usual to go either to the Republic or to England to publish a collection of poetry. That has changed substantially in the last decade, and about half the poets in *The New North* are published in Northern Ireland.

The size and prestige of several English presses means, of course, that publication in England can carry considerable critical weight for an Irish poet. Such British reputation naturally tends to dominate in the British view of Irish poetry, but it also flows back to Ireland and exerts a very powerful influence there, too. This asymmetry between British and Irish publishing in the formation of reputation across both islands is universally understood in the poetry worlds of both. It might be termed 'the elevation-suppression dynamic', and is hardly confined to poetry; it is an inescapable consequence of the disproportion between small and metropolitan cultures, and so has been felt with especial force in the North as a part of Britain. Whether this critical dynamic should be quite so readily assented to, and whether it will continue in the same way, has become more of an open question, now that 'the city state' publishes poetry as well.

There was only one problem with the trope of a third compact wave of Ulster poets: it never materialized. The North in the eighties and early nineties saw a complete dearth of first collections from those at home or abroad. Expectation seems to have outstripped apprenticeship. This may have had something to do with the absence of Northern poetry publishing, or the very notion of a dynastic succession, which came to seem as ossified as the Troubles themselves. Only from the mid-nineties, mainly with the poets assembled here, did a less obvious Northern 'publishing generation' achieve lift-off—whether from London, Dublin, Edinburgh, or Belfast.

It would be truer to say that what appeared was not so much a 'succession' as a 'scene'. This is the scene delineated by *The New North,* and it emerged from the Troubles into the new air of a new dispensation. Each of the poets here has staked a claim to some uninhabited space in the zodiac of Irish poetry. The island has been changed, changed utterly, since the outbreak of the Troubles; and its literary culture, North and South, perforce changed with it.

A certain critical over-mythologizing of Northern poetry due to its very distinction has long been a source of justifiable literary resentment in the South; but no equivalent trace of cultural exceptionalism is evident in the work assembled here. The sense of place, and of scene, has been 'normalized'. These poets are much more likely to be interested in new technology, ecology, Eastern Europe or bilingualism, than in any expected manifestation of 'the Northern issue'. In this, too, they have learnt from their Northern predecessors.

It is indeed the poetry of a new North.

—CHRIS AGEE

CLASSIC POEMS

SEAMUS HEANEY

[B. 1939]

BOGLAND

We have no prairies
To slice a big sun at evening—
Everywhere the eye concedes to
Encroaching horizon,

Is wooed into the cyclops' eye
Of a tarn. Our unfenced country
Is bog that keeps crusting
Between the sights of the sun.

They've taken the skeleton
Of the Great Irish Elk
Out of the peat, set it up
An astounding crate full of air.

Butter sunk under
More than a hundred years
Was recovered salty and white.
The ground itself is kind, black butter

Melting and opening underfoot,
Missing its last definition
By millions of years.
They'll never dig coal here,

Only the waterlogged trunks
Of great firs, soft as pulp.
Our pioneers keep striking
Inwards and downwards,

Every layer they strip
Seems camped on before.
The bogholes might be Atlantic seepage.
The wet centre is bottomless.

PUNISHMENT

I can feel the tug
of the halter at the nape
of her neck, the wind
on her naked front.

It blows her nipples
to amber beads,
it shakes the frail rigging
of her ribs.

I can see her drowned
body in the bog,
the weighing stone,
the floating rods and boughs.

Under which at first
she was a barked sapling
that is dug up
oak-bone, brain-firkin:

her shaved head
like a stubble of black corn,
her blindfold a soiled bandage,
her noose a ring

to store
the memories of love.
Little adulteress,
before they punished you

you were flaxen-haired,
undernourished, and your
tar-black face was beautiful.
My poor scapegoat,

I almost love you
but would have cast, I know,
the stones of silence.
I am the artful voyeur

of your brain's exposed
and darkened combs,
your muscles' webbing
and all your numbered bones:

I who have stood dumb
when your betraying sisters,
cauled in tar,
wept by the railings,

who would connive
in civilized outrage
yet understand the exact
and tribal, intimate revenge.

POSTSCRIPT

And some time make the time to drive out west
Into County Clare, along the Flaggy Shore,
In September or October, when the wind
And the light are working off each other
So that the ocean on one side is wild
With foam and glitter, and inland among stones
The surface of a slate-grey lake is lit
By the earthed lightning of a flock of swans,
Their feathers roughed and ruffling, white on white,

Their fully grown headstrong-looking heads
Tucked or cresting or busy underwater.
Useless to think you'll park and capture it
More thoroughly. You are neither here nor there,
A hurry through which known and strange things pass
As big soft buffetings come at the car sideways
And catch the heart off guard and blow it open.

DEREK MAHON

[B. 1941]

IN CARROWDORE CHURCHYARD

at the grave of Louis MacNeice

Your ashes will not stir, even on this high ground,
However the wind tugs, the headstones shake.
This plot is consecrated, for your sake,
To what lies in the future tense. You lie
Past tension now, and spring is coming round
Igniting flowers on the peninsula.

Your ashes will not fly, however the rough winds burst
Through the wild brambles and the reticent trees.
All we may ask of you we have; the rest
Is not for publication, will not be heard.
Maguire, I believe, suggested a blackbird
And over your grave a phrase from Euripides.

Which suits you down to the ground, like this churchyard
With its play of shadow, its humane perspective.
Locked in the winter's fist, these hills are hard

As nails, yet soft and feminine in their turn
When fingers open and the hedges burn.
This, you implied, is how we ought to live —

The ironical, loving crush of roses against snow,
Each fragile, solving ambiguity. So
From the pneumonia of the ditch, from the ague
Of the blind poet and the bombed-out town you bring
The all-clear to the empty holes of spring,
Rinsing the choked mud, keeping the colours new.

A DISUSED SHED IN CO. WEXFORD

Let them not forget us, the weak souls among
the asphodels. —SEFERIS, *Mythistorema*

for J. G. Farrell

Even now there are places where a thought might grow —
Peruvian mines, worked out and abandoned
To a slow clock of condensation,
An echo trapped for ever, and a flutter
Of wild flowers in the lift-shaft,
Indian compounds where the wind dances
And a door bangs with diminished confidence,
Lime crevices behind rippling rain-barrels,

Dog corners for bone burials;
And in a disused shed in Co. Wexford,

Deep in the grounds of a burnt-out hotel,
Among the bathtubs and the washbasins
A thousand mushrooms crowd to a keyhole.
This is the one star in their firmament
Or frames a star within a star.
What should they do there but desire?
So many days beyond the rhododendrons
With the world waltzing in its bowl of cloud,
They have learnt patience and silence
Listening to the rooks querulous in the high wood.

They have been waiting for us in a foetor
Of vegetable sweat since civil war days,
Since the gravel-crunching, interminable departure
Of the expropriated mycologist.
He never came back, and light since then
Is a keyhole rusting gently after rain.
Spiders have spun, flies dusted to mildew
And once a day, perhaps, they have heard something—
A trickle of masonry, a shout from the blue
Or a lorry changing gear at the end of the lane.

There have been deaths, the pale flesh flaking
Into the earth that nourished it;
And nightmares, born of these and the grim
Dominion of stale air and rank moisture.

Those nearest the door grow strong—
'Elbow room! Elbow room!'
The rest, dim in a twilight of crumbling
Utensils and broken pitchers, groaning
For their deliverance, have been so long
Expectant that there is left only the posture.

A half century, without visitors, in the dark—
Poor preparation for the cracking lock
And creak of hinges; magi, moonmen,
Powdery prisoners of the old regime,
Web-throated, stalked like triffids, racked by drought
And insomnia, only the ghost of a scream
At the flash-bulb firing-squad we wake them with
Shows there is life yet in their feverish forms.
Grown beyond nature now, soft food for worms,
They lift frail heads in gravity and good faith.

They are begging us, you see, in their wordless way,
To do something, to speak on their behalf
Or at least not to close the door again.
Lost people of Treblinka and Pompeii!
'Save us, save us,' they seem to say,
'Let the god not abandon us
Who have come so far in darkness and in pain.
We too had our lives to live.
You with your light meter and relaxed itinerary,
Let not our naive labours have been in vain!'

COURTYARDS IN DELFT

PIETER DE HOOCH, 1659

for Gordon Woods

Oblique light on the trite, on brick and tile —
Immaculate masonry, and everywhere that
Water tap, that broom and wooden pail
To keep it so. House-proud, the wives
Of artisans pursue their thrifty lives
Among scrubbed yards, modest but adequate.
Foliage is sparse, and clings; no breeze
Ruffles the trim composure of those trees.

No spinet-playing emblematic of
The harmonies and disharmonies of love,
No lewd fish, no fruit, no wide-eyed bird
About to fly its cage while a virgin
Listens to her seducer, mars the chaste
Perfection of the thing and the thing made.
Nothing is random, nothing goes to waste.
We miss the dirty dog, the fiery gin.

That girl with her back to us who waits
For her man to come home for his tea
Will wait till the paint disintegrates
And ruined dikes admit the esurient sea;

Yet this is life too, and the cracked
Outhouse door a verifiable fact
As vividly mnemonic as the sunlit
Railings that front the houses opposite.

I lived there as a boy and know the coal
Glittering in its shed, late-afternoon
Lambency informing the deal table,
The ceiling cradled in a radiant spoon.
I must be lying low in a room there,
A strange child with a taste for verse,
While my hard-nosed companions dream of fire
And sword upon parched veldt and fields of rain-swept gorse.

MICHAEL LONGLEY

[B. 1939]

THE BUTCHERS

When he had made sure there were no survivors in his house
And that all the suitors were dead, heaped in blood and dust
Like fish that fishermen with fine-meshed nets have hauled
Up gasping for salt water, evaporating in the sunshine,
Odysseus, spattered with muck and like a lion dripping blood
From his chest and cheeks after devouring a farmer's bullock,
Ordered the disloyal housemaids to sponge down the armchairs
And tables, while Telemachos, the oxherd and the swineherd
Scraped the floor with shovels, and then between the portico
And the roundhouse stretched a hawser and hanged the women
So none touched the ground with her toes, like long-winged thrushes
Or doves trapped in a mist-net across the thicket where they roost,
Their heads bobbing in a row, their feet twitching but not for long,
And when they had dragged Melanthios's corpse into the haggard
And cut off his nose and ears and cock and balls, a dog's dinner,
Odysseus, seeing the need for whitewash and disinfectant,
Fumigated the house and the outhouses, so that Hermes

Like a clergyman might wave the supernatural baton
With which he resurrects or hypnotises those he chooses,
And waken and round up the suitors' souls, and the housemaids',
Like bats gibbering in the nooks of their mysterious cave
When out of the clusters that dangle from the rocky ceiling
One of them drops and squeaks, so their souls were bat-squeaks
As they flittered after Hermes, their deliverer, who led them
Along the clammy sheughs, then past the oceanic streams
And the white rock, the sun's gatepost in that dreamy region,
Until they came to a bog-meadow full of bog-asphodels
Where the residents are ghosts or images of the dead.

PETALWORT

for Michael Viney

You want your ashes to swirl along the strand
At Thallabaun—amongst clockwork, approachable,
Circumambulatory sanderlings, crab shells,
Bladderwrack, phosphorescence at spring tide—

Around the burial mound's wind-and-wave-inspired
Vanishing act—through dowel-holes in the wreck—
Into bottles but without a message, only
Self-effacement in sand, additional eddies.

There's no such place as heaven, so let it be
The Carricknashinnagh shoal or Caher
Island where you honeymooned in a tent
Amid the pilgrim-fishermen's stations,

Your spillet disentangling and trailing off
Into the night, a ghost on every hook—dab
And flounder, thorny skate—at ebb tide you
Kneeling on watery sand to haul them in.

Let us choose for the wreath a flower so small
Even you haven't spotted on the dune-slack
Between Claggan and Lackakeely its rosette—
Petalwort: snail snack, angel's nosegay.

CEASEFIRE

I

Put in mind of his own father and moved to tears
Achilles took him by the hand and pushed the old king
Gently away, but Priam curled up at his feet and
Wept with him until their sadness filled the building.

II

Taking Hector's corpse into his own hands Achilles
Made sure it was washed and, for the old king's sake,
Laid out in uniform, ready for Priam to carry
Wrapped like a present home to Troy at daybreak.

III

When they had eaten together, it pleased them both
To stare at each other's beauty as lovers might,
Achilles built like a god, Priam good-looking still
And full of conversation, who earlier had sighed:

IV

'I get down on my knees and do what must be done
And kiss Achilles' hand, the killer of my son.'

CATHAL Ó SEARCAIGH

[B. 1956]

CAOINEADH

i gcuimhne mo mháthar

Chaoin mé na cuileatacha ar ucht mo mháthara
An lá a bhásaigh Mollie—peata de sheanchaora
Istigh i gcreagacha crochta na Beithí.
Á cuartú a bhí muid lá marbhánta samhraidh
Is brú anála orainn beirt ag dreasú na gcaorach
Siar ó na hailltreacha nuair a tímid an marfach
Sna beanna dodhreaptha. Préacháin dhubha ina scaotha
Á hithe ina beatha gur imigh an dé deiridh aisti
De chnead choscrach amháin is gan ionainn iarraidh
Tharrthála a thabhairt uirthi thíos sna scealpacha.
Ní thiocfaí mé a shásamh is an tocht ag teacht tríom;
D'fháisc lena hucht mé is í ag cásamh mo chaill liom
Go dtí gur chuireas an racht adaí ó íochtar mo chroí.
D'iompair abhaile mé ansin ar a guailneacha
Ag gealladh go ndéanfadh sí ceapairí arán préataí.

Inniu tá mo Theangaidh ag saothrú an bháis.
Ansacht na bhfilí—teangaidh ár n-aithreacha
Gafa i gcreagacha crochta na Faillí
Is gan ionainn í a tharrtháil le dásacht.
Cluinim na smeachannaí deireanacha
Is na héanacha creiche ag teacht go tapaidh,
A ngoba craosacha réidh chun feille.
Ó dá ligfeadh sí liú amháin gaile—liú catha

LAMENT

in memory of my mother

I cried on my mother's breast, cried sore
The day Mollie died, our old pet ewe
Trapped on a rockface up at Beithí.
It was sultry heat, we'd been looking for her,
Sweating and panting, driving sheep back
From the cliff-edge when we saw her attacked
On a ledge far down. Crows and more crows
Were eating at her. We heard the cries
But couldn't get near. She was ripped to death
As we suffered her terrible, wild, last breath
And my child's heart broke. I couldn't be calmed
No matter how much she'd tighten her arms
And gather me close. I just cried on
Till she hushed me at last with a piggyback
And the promise of treats of potato-cake.

To-day it's my language that's in its throes,
The poets' passion, my mothers' fathers'
Mothers' language, abandoned and trapped
On a fatal ledge that we won't attempt.
She's in agony, I can hear her heave
And gasp and struggle as they arrive,
The beaked and ravenous scavengers
Who are never far. Oh if only anger
Came howling wild out of her grief,

A chuirfeadh na creachadóirí chun reatha,
Ach seo í ag creathnú, seo í ag géilleadh;
Níl mo mháthair anseo le mé a shuaimhniú a thuilleadh
Is ní dhéanfaidh gealladh an phian a mhaolú.

PILLEADH AN DEORAÍ

Teach tréigthe roimhe anocht.
Ar an tairseach, faoi lom na gealaí, nocht,
scáile an tseanchrainn a chuir sé blianta ó shin.

TRIALL

do Rachel Brown

Triallfaidh mé le mo chrá amárach ar thearmann
anonn thar fhraoch na farraige;
óir chan fhuil fáil i reilig bhrocach na n-árasán
ar a bhfuil curtha anseo de m'óige.

If only she'd bare the teeth of her love
And rout the pack. But she's giving in,
She's quivering badly, my mother's gone
And promises now won't ease the pain.

[TRANSLATED BY SEAMUS HEANEY]

EXILE'S RETURN

He's back tonight to a deserted house.
On the doorstep, under a brilliant moon, a stark
shadow: the tree he planted years ago is an old tree.

[TRANSLATED BY SEAMUS HEANEY]

WILL TRAVEL

for Rachel Brown

To-morrow I travel on to a haven
Beyond the pitch and brawl of the sea:
The flats round here are a run-down graveyard
Where my young self walks like a nameless zombie.

Ansiúd thall tá seanteallach foscailte an chineáltais
agus tinidh chroíúil na fáilte;
ansiúd tá teangaidh sholásach ina cógas leighis
le léim a chur arís i mo shláinte.

Ó triallfaidh mé ar thearmann na coimirce anonn
agus dóchas ag bolgadh i mo sheolta;
áit a bhfaighidh mé goradh agus téarnaıh ann
ó shráideacha atá chomh fuar le tumba.

DO ISAAC ROSENBERG

Le bánú an lae agus muid ag teacht ar ais
i ndiaidh a bheith ag suirí i mbéal an uaignis
d'éirigh na fuiseoga as poill agus prochóga Phrochlais

agus chuimhnigh mé ortsa, a Isaac Rosenberg,
cathshuaite i dtailte treascartha na Fraince, ag éisteacht
le ceol sítheach na bhfuiseog le teacht an lae

agus tú ag pilleadh ar do champa, thar chnámha créachta
do chairde, ruaithne reatha na bpléascán, creathánach,
ag dcargadh an dorchadais ar pháirc an chatha.

In an open house over there, the hearth
Is the heart and soul of every welcome;
When I hear that candid, soothing accent
I'll be flush with health and my step will quicken.

O I'm travelling on to a sheltering haven
And hope is bellying out in my sail.
In a warmer place, I'll mend and be safe
From streets as cold as the wind round headstones.

[TRANSLATED BY SEAMUS HEANEY]

FOR ISAAC ROSENBERG

At dawn, we gave up our courting
out in the wilderness. Larks soared
from the bog-holes and hollows of Prochlais.

Then I thought of you, Isaac Rosenberg,
war-weary in the 'torn fields of France',
stunned by the siren larks, one dawn

as you returned to your camp over the ruined
bones of friends, shaken, with bombs
pouncing on the red and black battlefield.

Ag éisteacht le meidhir na bhfuiseog idir aer agus uisce
thaibhsigh do dhánta chugam thar thalamh eadrána na síoraíochta, líne,
ar líne, stadach, scáfar mar shaighdiúirí ó bhéal an áir

agus bhain siad an gus asam lena gcuntas ar an Uafás:
as duibheagán dubh na dtrinsí, as dóchas daortha na n-óg, as ár
agus anbhás, d'éirigh siad chugam as corrabhuais coinsiasa—

mise nach raibh ariamh sa bhearna bhaoil, nach dtug
ruathar mharfach thar an mhullach isteach sa chreach,
nár fhulaing i dtreascairt dhian na fola;

nach bhfaca saighdiúirí óga mar bheadh sopóga ann, caite
i gcuibhrinn mhéith an áir, boladh bréan an bháis
ag éirí ina phláigh ó bhláth feoite a n-óige;

nach raibh ar maos i nglár is i gclábar bhlár an chatha,
nár chaill mo mheabhair i bpléasc, nár mhothaigh an piléar
mar bheach thapaidh the ag diúl mhil fhiáin m'óige.

Ó ná hagair orm é, a Isaac Rosenberg, d'ainm a lua,
mise atá díonaithe i mo dhánta i ndún seo na Seirce
agus creach dhearg an chogaidh i gcroí na hEorpa go fóill.

Ach bhí mo chroí lasta le lúcháir agus caomhchruth álainn
mo leannán le mo thaobh, gach géag, gach alt, gach rinn,
gach ball de na ballaibh ó mhullach go talamh mo mhealladh,

The larks' joy between air and water
brought your poems across eternity's barricade, line
by line, stutteringly, scared, like soldiers in battle,

and they stopped me in my tracks with horror:
the dark pits of trenches, youth's smashed-up
hopes, the carnage wracked my conscience,

I who was never within an ounce of my life,
who never had to pile over the top and into battle,
who never lost out in any of the bloodshed,

I who never saw young soldiers torched
and dumped in an open field of slaughter,
their blighted bodies stinking with death,

I who was never plunged in the mud and mire,
never shell-shocked or stung by a bullet
sucking out my life like some crazy bee honey . . .

O, don't mind me, Isaac Rosenberg, calling you
from here, my safe-house of love poems,
while Europe still eats its heart out;

only mine was light with joy, my lover
beside me in all his glory, every limb,
joint, rim, every bit of him tempting me

sa chruth go gcreidim agus muid i mbachlainn a chéile
go bhfuil díon againn ar bhaol, go bhfuil an saol lán d'fhéile,
go bhfuil amhrán ár ngrá ina gheas ar gach aighneas.

Agus tá na fuiseoga ag rá an rud céanna liomsa a dúirt siad leatsa
sular cuireadh san aer tú, sular réabadh do chnámha—
Is fearr cumann agus ceol ná cogadh agus creach;

agus cé nach raibh mé ariamh i mbéal an chatha
agus cé nach bhfuil caite agam ach saol beag suarach, sabháilte,
ag daingniú mo choirnéil féin agus ag cúlú ó chúiseanna reatha;

ba mhaith liom a dhearbhú duitse, a fhile, a d'fhán go diongbháilte
i mbun d'fhocail, a labhair le lomchnámh na fírinne ó ár an chatha—
go bhfuil mise fosta ar thaobh an tSolais, fosta ar thaobh na Beatha.

OÍCHE

Cha raibh ann ach seomra beag suarach
i gceann de lóistíní oíche Shráid Ghardiner;
coincleach ar na ballaí, na braillíní buí agus brocach;
gan le cluinstin ach ochlán fada olagónach
na cathrach agus rúscam raindí na gcat

to believe that we're safe together,
that life is for feasting
and love wards off trouble.

The larks tell me what they told you,
before you were blown to pieces—
that love and music beat war and empire;

and though I've never been in action,
though I've had a safe, ordinary life,
looking after my own and keeping out of it,

I want to assure you, poet whose truth
was bared to the bones in World War I,
I too am on the side of light, and of life.

[TRANSLATED BY FRANK SEWELL]

NIGHT

it wasn't much of a room   one of those
B and B's off Gardiner Street
damp on the walls   the sheets yellow with grime
nothing to listen to but the slow moan of the drunkening
city and the racket from bin-hoking cats in the yard

ag déanamh raicit i mboscaí bruscair an chlóis;
ach ba chuma agus tusa, a rún na gile, sínte ar shlat
do dhroma, ar cholbha na leapa agus gan tuinte ort …

Agus tú ag dlúthú liom go docht, d'aoibhnigh do gháire
salachar an tseomra agus smúid oíche na sráide,
agus ansiúd ar sheanleabaidh lom na hainnise, bhí tú liom,
go huile agus go hiomlán, a ógánaigh chiúin an cheana.
Ansiúd ar an tseanleabaidh chruaidh, chnapánach úd
agus dombholadh an allais ag éirí ón éadach tais,
bhlais mé do bhéilín ró-dheas, do bheola te teolaí,
a chuir an fhuil ar fiuchadh ionam le barr teasbhaigh.

Bhí gach cead agam, an oíche úd, ar do chaoin chorp chaomh;
ar ghile cúr séidthe do bhoilg; ar do bhaill bheatha
a ba chumhra ná úllaí fomhair bheadh i dtaiscigh le ráithe;
ar mhaolchnocáin mhíne do mhásaí, ar bhoige liom go mór iad
faoi mo láimh, ná leithead d'éadaigh sróil, a mbeadh tomhas
den tsíoda ina thiúis … Anois agus mé mo luí
anseo liom féin i leabaidh léin an díomhaointis
tá mé ar tí pléascadh aríst le pléisiúr … le tocht

ag cuimhniú ortsa, a ógánaigh álainn, deargnocht
a d'aoibhnigh an oíche domh … ocht mbliana déag ó shin, anocht.

but so what? weren't you lying flat on your back
on the edge of the bed   undressed to the nines?

and you clung to me so tight   your laugh transforming
the dirty room and murky night outside
to bliss   there on the wreck of a bed   you
in all your pow and glory   my quiet young lover
there on that hard hurting bed with stale
sweat rising from the damp sheet   your warm
comforting lips kissed my blood alight.

that night   I could do anything with your slender-smooth body
your belly bright as a foaming wave   and below—
more tempting than autumn apples a season stored
mine were the rolling drumlins of your cheeks   soft
under my hand and light as the scantiest silk   now
alone   on a no-such-lucky bed
in pain   in joy   I remember you   beautiful   naked

transforming my night   eighteen years ago   tonight

[TRANSLATED BY FRANK SEWELL]

I GCEANN MO THRÍ BLIANA A BHÍ MÉ

do Anraí Mac Giolla Chomhaill

'Sin clábar! Clábar cáidheach,
a chuilcigh,' a dúirt m'athair go bagrach
agus mé ag slupairt go súgach
i ndíobhóg os cionn an bhóthair.
'Amach leat as do chuid clábair
sula ndéanfar tú a clonáil!'

Ach choinnigh mé ag spágáil agus ag splaiseáil
agus ag scairtigh le lúcháir:
'Clábar! Clábar! Seo mo chuid clábair!'
Cé nár chiallaigh an focal faic i mo mheabhair
go dtí gur mhothaigh mé i mo bhuataisí glugar
agus trí gach uile líbín de mo cheirteacha
creathanna fuachta na tuisceana.

A chlábar na cinniúna, bháigh tú mo chnámha.

CLABBER: THE POET AT THREE YEARS

'That's clabber! Clutching clabber
sucks caddies down,' said my father harshly
while I was stomping happily
in the ditch on the side of the road.
'Climb out of that clabber pit
before you catch your death of it!'

But I went on splattering and splashing,
and scattering whoops of joy:
'Clabber! Clabber! I belong to it,'
although the word meant nothing to me
until I heard a squelch in my wellies
and felt through every fibre of my duds
the cold tremors of awakening knowledge.

O elected clabber, you chilled me to the bone.

[TRANSLATED BY JOHN MONTAGUE]

BEAN AN tSLÉIBHE

do Bhríd, Mhaighréad agus Shorcha

Bhí féith na feola inti ach fosta féith an ghrinn
agus in ainneoin go raibh sí mantach agus mórmhionnach
ní raibh sí riamh gruama nó grusach linn
nuair a bhíodh sinn thuas aici ar an Domhnach,
is dhéanadh sí splais tae dúinn os cionn na gríosaí,
is í ag cur spleoid ar seo, is spréadh ar siúd go teasaí.

Is ba mhinic í ag gearán fán *tseanbhugger* de *ghauger*
a ghearr siar í sa phinsean is a d'fhág í ar an bheagán
cionn is go raibh bó i mbéal beirthe aici sa bhóitheach
cúpla bearach ar féarach agus dornán caorach
agus í ag trácht ar an eachtra deireadh sí go feargach:
'Sa tír seo tugtar na *crusts* is cruaidhe don té atá mantach.'

Is chuidíodh muid léi i dtólamh ar an Domhnach
aoileach na seachtaine a chartadh as an bhóitheach,
is nuair a bhíodh muid ag déanamh faillí inár ngnaithe,
ag bobaireacht ar chúl a cinn is ag broimnigh,
deireadh sí, 'Á cuirigí séip oraibh féin a chailleacha,
ní leasóidh broim an talamh san earrach.'

'Bhfuil *jizz* ar bith ionaibh, a bhuachaillí?' a deireadh sí
nuair a bhíodh leisc orainn easaontú lena tuairimí.
'Oró tá sibh chomh bómánta le huain óga an earraigh,

MOUNTAIN WOMAN

for Bríd, Maighréad and Sorcha

She was fleshy but funny, and though
she swore through the gaps in her teeth,
she was never gruff or gloomy with us
when we called round on Sundays
for a 'splash' of tea made over the fire
as she darn-blasted this, that and the other.

She'd give off about the 'bugger of an inspector'
who cut her pension down to even less
just 'cos she'd a cow in the byre near calving,
a few heifers out to grass and a clatter of sheep;
when she talked of this affront, she'd say,
'when you've no teeth, you get crusts in this country.'

We always helped her out on Sundays,
clearing a week-load of dung from the byre
and when we took our time about our work,
messing about and letting off behind her back,
she'd say, 'c'mon, lads, put a step on it,
what'll yez reap if yez sow a fart?

Have yez any jizz in yez at all, boys?,'
she'd say when we ducked a dispute with her.
'Aah, yez are as daft as them spring lambs,

ach sin an rud atá na sagairt is na TDs a iarraidh,
is nuair a thiocfas sibhse i méadaíocht, a bhuachaillí,
ní bheidh moill ar bith orthu sibh a thiomáint mar chaoirigh.'

Chothaigh sí í féin ansiúd mar a dhéanfadh crann
ag feo is ag fás de réir an tséasúir a bhí ann.
'Ní ag aoisiú atá mé,' a deireadh sí 'ach ag apú,'
is mar shíolta thitfeadh a briathra in úir mhéith m'aigne
is nuair a shnaidhmeadh sí a géaga thart orm go teann
mhothaínn an gheir—fáinní fáis a colainne.

'Níl crann sna flaithis níos airde ná Crann na Foighde',
a deireadh sí agus í ag foighneamh go fulangach leis an bhás
a bhí ag lomadh agus ag creachadh a géaga gan spás.
Anois cuirim Aifreann lena hanam ó am go ham i gcuimhne
ar an toradh a bhronn sí orm ó Chrann na hAithne
agus mar a déarfadh sí féin dá mbeadh sí ina beathaidh,

'Is fearr cogar sa chúirt ná scread ar an tsliabh, a thaiscidh.'

just the way the priests and politicians want yez
and when yez are big enough, lads,
they'll have no trouble herding yez like sheep.'

She stood her ground like an old tree,
growing or drooping depending on the season.
'I'm not aging,' she'd say, 'but ripening.'
Her words fell like seeds on my young mind
and when she'd wrap her arms tight around me,
I felt her breadth — the growth-rings of her body.

'The highest tree in heaven is Patience,'
she said, bravely bearing up to death
as it hurt and hacked her limbs relentlessly.
Sometimes I have a Mass said in memory
of the fruit she gave me from the tree of knowledge.
As she would say herself, if she were around:

'a soft word in the right ear gets heard.'

[TRANSLATED BY FRANK SEWELL]

DO JACK KEROUAC

do Shéamas de Bláca

The only people for me are the mad ones, the ones who are mad to live,
mad to talk, mad to be saved, desirous of everything at the same time,
the ones who never yawn or say a commonplace thing but burn, burn
like fabulous yellow roman candles. [SLÍOCHT AS *On the Road*]

Ag sioscadh trí do shaothar anocht tháinig leoithne na cuimhne
    chugam ó gach leathanach.
Athmhúsclaíodh m'óige is mhothaigh mé ag éirí ionam an *beat*
    brionglóideach a bhí ag déanamh aithrise ort i dtús na seachtóidí.
1973. Bhi mé *hook*áilte ort. Lá i ndiaidh lae fuair mé *shot* inspioráide
    ó do shaothar a ghealaigh m'aigne is a shín mo shamhlaíocht.
Ní Mín 'a Leá ná Fána Bhuí a bhí á fheiceáil agam an t-am adaí ach
    machairí Nebraska agus táilte fearaigh Iowa.
Agus nuair a thagadh na *bliú*nanna orm ní bealach na Bealtaine a
    bhí romham amach ach mórbhealach de chuid Mheiriceá.
'Hey man you gotta stay high,' a déarfainn le mo chara agus muid ag
    *freak*áil trí Chailifornia Chill Ulta isteach go Frisco an Fhál
    Charraigh.

Tá do leabhar ina luí druidte ar m'ucht ach faoi chraiceann an
    chlúdaigh tá do chroí ag preabadaigh i bhféitheog gach focail.
Oh man mothaím aris, na *higheanna* adaí ar Himiléithe na hóige:
Ó chósta go cósta thriall muid le chéile, saonta, spleodrach,
    místiúrtha;

LET'S HIT THE ROAD, JACK

for Seamas de Blaca

The only people for me are the mad ones, the ones who are mad to live,
mad to talk, mad to be saved, desirous of everything at the same time,
the ones who never yawn or say a commonplace thing but burn,
burn like fabulous yellow roman candles. [FROM *On the Road*]

Short-cutting through your trail tonight,
memory revved at every stage;
youth harleyed and sent me again
on the dreambeat pulse of the early 70s.
Yeah, nineteen seventy-three!
Hooked, lined and sinkered on the shots
you gave me like gas to blow my mind,
I saw home turn plainly to Nebraska,
Fána Bhuí to the green grass of Iowa;
and, when the blues came belting down,
Bealtaine Road was an open freeway;
Hey man you gotta stay high, we'd say,
Californicating Cill Ulta, Friscying Falcarragh.

Your book lies closed on my chest
but, under the covers, your heartbeat
pulses in time to every word.
Oh, man! I still feel the wild highs,
the Himalayas of youth as we coasted

Oilithreacht ordóige ó Nua-Eabhrac go Frisco agus as sin go Cathair
Mheicsiceo;
Beat buile inár mbeatha. Spregtha. Ag bladmadh síos bóithre i
gCadillacs ghasta ag sciorradh thar íor na céille ar eiteoga na
m*bennies.*
Thuasnaigh muid teorainneacha agus thrasnaigh muid taibhrithe.

Cheiliúraigh muid gach casadh ar bhealach ár mbeatha, *binge*anna
agus
bráithreachas ó Bhrooklyn go Berkeley, *booze, bop* agus Búdachas;
Éigse na hÁise; sreangscéalta as an tsíoraíocht ar na Sierras;
marijuana agus misteachas i Meicsiceo; brionglóidí buile i
mBixby Canyon.

Rinne muid Oirféas as gach *orifice*.

Ó is cuimhneach liom é go léir, a Jack, an chaint is an cuartú.
Ba tusa bard beoshúileach na mbóithre, ar thóir na foirfeachta,
ar thóir na bhFlaitheas.
Is cé nach bhfuil aon aicearra chuig na Déithe, a deirtear, d'éirigh
leatsa slí a aimsiú in amantaí nuair a d'fheistigh tú úim adhainte
ar Niagara d'aigne le *dope* is le diagacht.
Is i mBomaite sin na Buile gineadh solas a thug spléachadh duit ar
an tSíoraíocht,
Is a threoraigh 'na bhaile tú, tá súil agam, lá do bháis chuig
Whitman, Proust agus Rimbaud.

Tá mo bhealach féin romham amach . . . '*a road that ah zigzags all
over creation. Yeah man! Ain't nowhere else it can go. Right!*'

the coasts together, innocents abroad,
unleashed and up-for-it, thumbing
from NYC to Frisco and on
to Mexico, a wild beat
in our veins and brains. Inspired. Hot-wired.
Cadillaccellerating down roads,
skidding out of our brains on *bennies*,
borders passed like dreams as we tuned in
and turned on to life's freeway, bingeing
and buddying from Brooklyn to Berkeley
on booze, bop and Buddhism, the wisdom
of the East, telegrams from eternity
over the Sierras, marijuana
and mysticism in Mexico,
crazy dreams in Bixby canyon.
Oh Jack, we made an Orpheus
of every orifice . . .

Man, I remember every speel of the hunt
as you wide-eyed the roads for perfection,
for heaven. And though they'd say there's no
speedway to the gods, you made in-roads,
sometimes transfixing your Niagara mind,
scaling the chords between pot and prayer.
Then the lightning struck, and you
glimpsed eternity enough, I hope,
to join Whitman, Proust and Rimbaud.

My own long and winding road
leads, like yours, *all over creation*.

Agus lá inteacht ar bhealach na seanaoise is na scoilteacha
Nó lá níos cóngaraí do bhaile, b'fhéidir,
Sroichfidh mé Croisbhealach na Cinniúna is beidh an Bás romham
    ansin,
Treoraí tíriúil le mé a thabhairt thar teorainn,
Is ansin, *goddammit* a Jack, beidh muid beirt ag síobshiúl sa
                         tSíoraíocht.

AN TOBAR

do Mháire Mhac an tSaoi

'Cuirfidh sé brí ionat agus beatha,'
arsa sean-Bhríd, faghairt ina súile
ag tabhairt babhla fíoruisce chugam
as an tobar is glaine i nGleann an Átha.
Tobar a coinníodh go slachtmhar
ó ghlúin go glúin, oidhreacht
luachmhar an teaghlaigh
cuachta istigh i gclúid foscaidh,
claí cosanta ina thimpeall
leac chumhdaigh ar a bhéal.

Yeah man! Ain't nowhere else it can go.
And when I'm on my last legs,
in old age or sooner than I think,
I'll check out Death down at the crossroads,
have him smuggle me over the border,
then, goddammit Jack, we'll both
hitchhike, ah, the zigzag roads of heaven.

[TRANSLATED BY FRANK SEWELL]

THE WELL

for Máire Mhac an tSaoi

'That'll put the jizz back in you,'
said old Brid, her eyes glinting,
as she handed me a bowl of real water
from the purest well in Gleann an Atha.
A well kept sweet and neat
by her people's people, the precious
legacy of the household,
tucked away in a nook,
a ditch around it for protection,
a flagstone on its mouth.

Agus mé ag teacht i méadaíocht
anseo i dtús na seascaidí
ní raibh teach sa chomharsanacht
gan a mhacasamhail de thobar,
óir cúis mhaíte ag achan duine
an t-am adaí a fholláine is a fhionnuaire
a choinníodh sé tobar a mhuintire:
ní ligfí sceo air ná smál
is dá mbeadh rian na ruamheirge
le feiceáil ann, le buicéad stáin
dhéanfaí é a thaoscadh ar an bhall
is gach ráithe lena choinneáil folláin
chumhraítí é le haol áithe.

Uisce beo bíogúil, fíoruisce glé
a d'fhoinsigh i dtobar ár dteaghlaigh.
I gcannaí agus i gcrúiscíní
thóg said é lá i ndiaidh lae
agus nuair a bhíodh íota tarta orthu
i mbrothall an tsamhraidh
thugadh fliuchadh agus fuarú daofa
i bpáirceanna agus i bportaigh.
Deoch íce a bhí ann fosta
a chuir ag preabadaigh iad le haoibhneas
agus mar uisce ionnalta
d'fhreastail ar a gcás ó bhreith go bás.

Ach le fada tá uisce reatha
ag fiaradh chugainn isteach

Here, in the early sixties
just as I came into my strength
there wasn't a house in the district
without a well like this. Everyone
so proud of how sweet and cool
they kept the family well. They'd allow
no glut or glar to gather in it
and a trace of rust was reason
enough to bail it out at once with tin
buckets. Each quarter day without
fail, they'd kiln-lime it sweet.

The lucid gush of a true spring
burst and plashed from my people's well.
When we were consumed by thirst
and struck with summer's sweat
we took it daily by bowl and pitcher.
It slacked and cooled us in fields
and bog. It throbbed through us
like a tonic — gave us life and laughter.
It washed us all, from the infant's
first bath to the corpse's last cleaning.

But for a long time now there is a snake
of pipe that sneaks in from distant hills
and in every kitchen, both sides
of the glen, water spits from a tap;
bitter water without spark

ó chnoic i bhfad uainn
is i ngach cisteanach
ar dhá thaobh an ghleanna
scairdeann uisce as sconna
uisce lom gan loinnir
a bhfuil blas searbh súlaigh air
is i measc mo dhaoine
tá tobar an fhíoruisce ag dul i ndíchuimhne.

'Is doiligh tobar a aimsiú faoi láthair,'
arsa Bríd, ag líonadh an bhabhla athuair.
'Tá siad folaithe i bhfeagacha agus i bhféar,
tachtaithe ag caileannógach agus cuiscreach,
ach in ainneoin na neamhairde go léir
níor chaill siad a dhath den tseanmhianach.
Aimsigh do thobar féin, a chroí,
óir tá am an anáis romhainn amach:
Caithfear pilleadh arís ar na foinsí.'

that leaves a bad taste in the mouth
and among my people
the real well is being forgotten.

'It's hard to find a well these days,'
said old Bríd, filling up my bowl again.
'They're hiding in rushes and juking in grass,
all choked up and clatty with scum
but for all the neglect they get
their mettle is still true.
Look for your own well, pet,
for there's a hardtime coming.
There will have to be a going back to sources.'

[TRANSLATED BY THE AUTHOR]

JEAN BLEAKNEY

[B. 1956]

IN MEMORIAM

If it's over, *let it be over*,
how can we forget? We should not forget
the years that were rank with abscissions;
the days when our unuttered shame
was as stagnant as the cut flowers
blackening under cellophane;
the autumn when streets and townlands shrank
to funeral gatherings—as tightly concentric
as the petals of chrysanthemums;
the hopeless sense of everything falling away
except the leaves, the reddening leaves.

THE VIEW FROM CARRAN WEST

Only now, now that the leaves have fallen,
can we measure the season's growth
in lengths of bright untainted bark.

Only now, now that autumn's almost over,
can we see beyond to the deepening lough
where a summer sun rolled down the mountainside
to Inishtemple, Inishmean and Inisheher.

Except that now, now the view from the house
is opening up to winter, the mountain
has stolen the sun; the lough is blackening
and a storm from the west has set her heart
on littering the shore with broken branches.

STARGAZING FOR FEMINISTS

Well proud of the horizon,
undressed to kill, the both of them
—full moon all bosomy white
and Venus, faceted and glittery,
as bold as you like;
admiring one another
as well they might
and amplified because of it.

Between, caught up in the cross-talk,
Orion: Mighty Hunter, skirt-chaser,
tormentor of the Pleiades
—but not such a big lad tonight.
As body outlines go
he's a bit splayed out,
a bit of a John Doe,
now that the girls are back in town.

ALWAYS

Even after the narrative dwindles
(as it will, it surely will) there'll be
elaborations and enumerations:
the odd avalanche of sky-detail;
March's headcount of magnolia buds
and later, wind-corralled against red brick,
the autumn-bruckle chestnut leaves;
their hoard of spiny apples—still intact?
Or scuffled down to shells? For seasons being
not wholly reliable indices
there'll always be some or other pageant
to report—something heartfelt, extant.

FROM A TRAIN IN HUNGARY

Incorrigible sunworshippers,
their discreet swivellings
imperceptible as radio telescope dishes,
they stare out the sun
(or the clouds covering it)
from dawn to dusk, until
full flowered, stiff necked
—their stems grown woody—
they fix their gaze on sunrise.

Consider the awkward interregnum:
the days when those still turning
swing to face their neighbours—
those odd evenings of congress
when east meets west—
each roguc bloom as ill-prepared,
as shy of inquisitive glances
as a tourist on this Intercity
fumbling for a phrase book
or that one remembered word
—*kurssurnurm*—
who turns to face the window,
its achingly familiar greens,
a few glimpsed storks,
then hours and hours
—or so it seems—of sunflowers.

köszönöm (kurssurnurm): thank you

THE FAIRYTALE LAND OF UM

Between the supercilious litany of ultra
and the negative hordes of un
is the magical realism of Um.
Complete with sense of journey

(from the . . . um . . . hesitant opening
to the self-assurance of umpteen);
and sense of place—Central Italy
with its earth of red-brown oxides
and good-verus-evil flora of cow parsley,
angelica, sweet cicely, hemlock and giant hogweed
whose umbel flower parts are spoked and rayed
as umbrellas. Rain is assumed . . . or sun.
So is conflict: visors, shields and umiaks
(open boats crewed by Inuit women)
not to mention slaughtered deer and umble pie.
Eclipsed, in minor roles, the umpire
and that Germanic vowel modifier.
Not so, the flapping stork-like umbrette:
a roc of a bird and in the wrong continent.
Not so, that lacy-leafed jungle of umbellifers
adumbrating each other's flat-topped inflorescences,
in whose shadowy undergrowth squats umbrage,
that navel-gazing familiar:
umbrage, the giving and taking of it.

THE POET'S IVY

One kind has a black seed and another the colour of saffron. The latter
is used by poets for their wreaths and its leaves are not so dark in colour.
—*Natural History of Pliny* (AD 22–79)

So

prized,

that it crowned

the winners of poetry

contests, Hedera *poetica*—

elaborated in the eighteenth century

to Hedera *poetica baccis luteis*, The Yellow

Archipelagian Ivy—has since been downwardly

revised through Hedera *helix* ssp. *poetarum* and

Hedera *helix* var. *poetarum* to, within the last ten years,

the lowest botanical rank: Hedera *helix* f. *poetarum*.

Distinguished merely by dullish orange berries

and lightish green leaves, it is rarely sought

and seldom offered.

P

o

e

t

s,

on

the

other

hand,

though

seldom sought,

are as frequently encountered,

as detachable from their lofty ambitions

as Hedera *helix*, the common hedgerow ivy,

and its whole gallery of

subspecies, varieties and

f

o

r

m

s.

DENATURATION

Taken on its own, the fickle doorbell
has no particular score to settle
(a reluctant clapper? an ill-at-ease dome?)
were it not part of a whole syndrome:
the stubborn gate; flaking paint; cotoneaster
camouflaging the house number.
Which is not to say the occupant
doesn't have (to hand) lubricant,

secateurs, paint scraper, an up-to-date
shade card known by heart.
It's all part of the same deferral
that leaves hanging baskets vulnerable;
although, according to a botanist,
for most plants, short-term wilt
is really a *protective* mechanism.
But surely every biological system
has its limits? There's no going back
for egg white once it's hit the fat.
Yet, some people seem determined to stretch, to redefine
those limits. Why are they so inclined?

RECUPERATION

Whether to put the tulips or the lilies
centre-table is the day's dilemma.
Whether to consolidate . . . except

tulips are tulips. Too self-possessed
to cohabit. The lilies were there first.
They're already bunched: oriental

with still-in-bud *longiflorum*.
Should the new usurp? Darlings,
I've come over all Mrs Dalloway;

I'm dreamily Virginia-tinged in this
post-anaesthesia lassitude. Day 4:
even flower placement defeats me.

It's as if my brain's shrink-wrapped;
that or I'm sitting on its doorstep
waiting for somebody else's key.

See how cut tulips right themselves
taking their bearings less
from light than from gravity.

DEDUCTION

Not the whitefly, nor the vine weevil,
nor the mealy bug, nor the scale insect,
nor woolly aphid, nor other viviparous aphid,
nor spider mite, nor any sap-sucker *per se*
but rather, one senses, the leaf miner
– lover of lamellae and interstices;
burrower between the host leaf's
top and bottom sheets — *yes*,
the leaf miner, with it green-tinted
soft-focus view of the garden;
engineer of the long and winding
blister of its own meanderings . . .
least among pests, the leaf miner is surely
the apprentice poet of the piece.

CHRIS AGEE

[B. 1956]

MUSHROOMING

Nothing stills the woods to silence
like the aftermath of rains, the meadow-crickets quenched,
the boughs and saplings of birch and pine

dropping their desultory *plops*, shining
here and there with sunshafts from parted cloud
whose mottle on moist leaf-litter

is a moss of light. This is the inspired time
the Greeks felt the mystery of Zeus,
the lightning's muse

in the dark labour of fungi. Vicarious as the uprush
of poetry, the delicate caps of mushrooms
thrust through the earth's rot, half-masked by a layer of leaves,

by mossy vestiges of treetrunks
holed by woodpeckers,
birch-logs broken-backed like tumbled pillars of alabaster,

branches fallen in autumn
where Indian pipe sprouts on bark
and a meandering wall is Frost's art

like lichen on the stones of Nineveh. A paradise of phalloi
mushrooming in damp, all named and infused
by the genius of fieldwork,

in the Eden of amateur mycology:
Chanterelle, Thimble-cap, Velvet-footed Pax,
the ochre, Latinate splendour

of *Voluminous Milky*
with its fishstink and profusion of latex:
each under-cap a haven for slugs,

a language all its own,
neither prose nor song,
not animal, yet not quite plant,

their svelte ethereal flesh
and tinges of extraordinary colour
the Zen of life,

a quickening blush of humus
in one-day miracles of the world's design
like haikus in the woodland epic of birth and decay.

LOON CALL

Its black head might surface midafternoon off a dock
of planks weathered gray as wasp's nest: or its call
sound hauntingly across the placid light of Squam

at duskfall, the sky the inside of a seashell: catching me
at a desk in lamplight, back to a screendoor
filled with the endless rattle-shake of summer insects:

standing, gazing upwards in tall meadow grass
shadowed with moonlight, in thrall to the constellations
and the galaxy-mantle of the Milky Way: in ferny birchwoods

aswim with sun-mottle on lichened boulders: reminding me,
like the Möbius of thought turned on itself,
of the life of the moment it mortalizes.

PORT OF BELFAST

Hung on a wall of Calvinist stars,
the moon is a mottled goatskin bodhrán,
a vellum of weathered light
above the fog and frost of Lagan dips.

AT BETHLEHEM NURSERY

in memory of Miriam

The frost this morning was thick, Byzantine,
Coating an infinite wicker of grass leaves, blades of daffodil,
Old November leaves curled like lips of conch,
Side-view mirror fingered clear in the early morning

Eternally new. Quintessential Irish chill, unvanquished bluish-white
Under sleepers of shadow on sun-warmed verges,
The visitation, the annunciation of night—fog's delicate lacework
Breathed out by the Gulf Stream's circumpolar Ariel.

OFFING

That sun, a moon almost: I remember it like a bindi
On the cool brow of a porcelain buddha, a red spot

In the mist of dusk. That place, that microcosmos,
The clean lines of clapboard, the crimson cupola,

Summers in New England, light in August,
What can I say? What can you say of life?

That I was there, that it was here. That place
I first felt its deep offing, that porch I walked from,

The gingerbread of the spartan Cottage,
The shuffleboard, the lawn's two iron deer

Asperged with dew, a Wednesday's sixties line-dance,
Deck rockers under the trestle of stars, gin rummy

In the Sun Room. On down the hill rippling through
To the swans on the Spring House pond,

A teardrop on the brow of the Bluffs,
Deep in cornflowers and Queen Anne's lace.

That place I still return to, fresh as ever,
The clatter of dishes, the old Polish cook

With his broken English and wild eyes,
The waitresses in white, meals *al fresco*

On the laundry landing, *circa* '71.
Sails in the offing, our Shack and psychedelic Barn

Out back towards the wall-quilt and grasses
Sprinkled with cornflowers and Queen Anne's lace.

Out for a break from the dinner din.
In the stillness, the empty Annex, a red disc sinking

Like the buoy of crepuscule. That time. That place
I spent some misspent youth. That porch. That dew.

FIRST LIGHT

One begins not knowing
what the mind will beachcomb from the radiant flux
of things in the intertidal zone, what the combers

have left at first light:
a sawn stump with three worn nodes,
a buoy in wrack, a corncob, a dead ray:

the subtle patinas of the bluffs
beetled by bay and bittersweet,
riddled by the cliff-dwellings of swallows:

dark glistening surf
occasioned by trails of mackerel-cloud:
the vast abstraction

of dry smooth shingle-stones infinitely variable
under foot. Or, finally, brilliant indigo-and-seagreen
under a clearing sky. You have quickstepped thus

in spirit, from stepping-stone to stepping-stone
as if some surefooted Chinese boatman
leaping nimbly athwart junk-to-junk at a mooring—

though unable to say, looking back,
should you ask yourself, how exactly you traversed
that hour's crescent of foaming sand and shingle-bank.

REQUIEM

Something had turned me back. Broken stone. Ochre and lime
Leaves in the pockmark of a mortarsplash. I paused

To marvel at the chaos that composed them
Impasted in hoarfrost like sperms or dead souls frozen

In the liquid oxygen of time. Then back again
To the smoothness on a mosque's threshold, a revenant

Drifting on in the first flurries of Friday afternoon,
Windless and lightweight, sifting down in grey silence,

I walk on past shawled faces in an old Yugoslav café,
Bread smells and a glimpse of loaves, jars stacked pyramidal

As in Russia, crossing Habsburg tramlines to the market stalls
Where legs and shoe leather move round the small splash

That, invisible, unsought, I wince at. Walnuts, cabbages, tangerines:
Onions, apples, peppers, honeycomb: bowls of cheese, sunflower seeds:

Beautiful, spartan Arcimboldo, where Sarajevo snow is falling, falling . . .
Is ash falling into the next century.

SEBALD

On and off, I had been musing about vistas
Of simultaneity: the continuum between, say,

In a natural sense, fresh graves in Afghanistan
And the abysmal plain on the Marianas Trench

Lit by the spectral traceries of bioluminescence; or,
In the social, sipping coffee as Srebrenica happened

In waves of twenty-plus. How — at any one time — everything
Is happening in a single world-image like tens of millions

Of words in the Babel of thousands of tongues coexisting
In its archive of consciousness. That interior Friday

In the Year of the Buddhas, it might have happened
As I paused for a moment at a window over Royal Avenue

Or collected my daughter's last photographs amid the sad
Crepuscule of the framing shop. Now, over coffee, reading

Of *seiceamóir* and *cuileann* in *Trees of Ireland*,
I think of his radiant endings: *a last glimpse of the land*

now being lost forever and *reaching the town*
as evening began to fall: and hope

His noble German span and hers in miniature
Are travelling forever into the dark land of eternal light.

ALPINE INTERLUDE

When we reached the mountain bog in the saddle
Of Jackson, and saw the heads of thousands
Of cotton sedge trembling and bobbing, letting go

Their fleecy tufts like thistledown in Ireland
Over archipelagos of blackbrown peat sediment—
I thought, after a while, of those days in Kosovo: life

Essential in its passing, its beauty, its tragedy. But first
Pausing long trail minutes, the boy becalmed on
Planks of the bog bridge, seeing mountain cranberry,

Pale laurel, Canada mayflower, windy Appalachian bog
Rimmed by Labrador tea, the sweetness of the moment
Reminded me of Miriam's life, its brevity and softness,

Its summery interlude, its sunniness stretching
Out to the unending dark dwarf balsam fir-trees
And the great universe bowl of the White Mountains

In sheer airy blue outline, the cumuli sailing in
Puffs of snapdragon and Hiroshima ... with which,
Nonetheless, in the mind's eye, her time seemed one.

IN PRVO SELO

In the tradition of the place, once or more a summer,
We return to our evergreen Žrnovo door
And find hung, leant or left round the bronzed handle
Or smoothed limestone threshold, some ghost-token
Of a visitor—a bow of straw, or sheer headscarf,
Or terrace cushion, or wildflower or bough plucked
Nearby at a moment's notice. Sometimes, too, a gift
Materializes. Some tomatoes perhaps, or grappa
In a second-hand bottle, maybe a book or compote,
Lavender and oregano out of the adjacent fields,
Small cakes from a neighbour's kitchen. And if
Merely a folded piece of paper, always with neither
Name nor note. Thus out of this village silence
Immemorial as Anonymous, you come to realise
You're expected to intuit whoever it might have been
Who wished or needed seeing you at the dog day's
Missed periphery. Though once in a blue moon too,
The gift-giver or visit, like a ghost guested all summer,
Asked after, stays unknown despite the guesswork.

SUMMER PLUMS

In the valley before Srebrenica the corn was the tallest
I've ever seen. Someone was reaping by sickle
what looked like lavender. Another was scything silage.
Several places, women in kerchiefs and pantaloons
were sat on grass before their houses, looking out.
Low steep hills ringed the valley

with thick woods. There were domed Bosnian
haystacks pinnacled with poles and shells of ruined houses
colonized by undergrowth. It seemed right to return
to renew fields and gardens amid beckoning ghosts
of family and neighbours. A cow was led
on a rope by an old woman in the same dress

and a girl in shorts walked the road
to Potočari. A windfall of apples was
down in an orchard and silken plums scattered
on a forested lane. Two headstones stood
in a cornfield like a summer host
of thousands of splendid ears.

MOYRA DONALDSON

[B. 1956]

INFIDELITIES

After he'd gone,
she found money in the sheets,
fallen when he pulled his trousers off.
Gathering the coins into a small pile
she set them on the window ledge.
They sat, gathering dust, guilt,
until one day her husband
scooped them into his pocket.
Small change for a call
he couldn't make from the house.

OUT OF THE ORDINARY

Until now I had no faith to lose.
Then your belief taught me it is
ordinary things that speak the language
I once thought only God would use.
Chaos still rolls beyond our little fences,
and the wrong place is always only
a split second away. The cell can mutate,
brakes fail, and we must take our chances.

You hold off fear with small certainties,
and rhythmical days where each minute

flows easy to the next and into sleep.
Wakening with you I am at ease.
Few declarations, more steadfastness,
little considerations I so nearly missed.

PLANTER

My brother is a lean white shadow in the early morning light,
unspoken things
have kept him thin, despite his wife's attempts to fatten him on love.

From the window I watch him walk his fields to their furthest edges,
where the deer graze.
He has dug himself a place, refused to be the seed on stony ground

and with a farmer's faith, he harvests himself against winter,
each winnowing
yielding the new history that he is planting in his children's hearts.

'82–'89

It was a crooked time —

that's how it happened, that she fell for the crooked man
and went to live with him in his little crooked house

where every night she fed his crooked cat
as he counted his crooked sixpences into a purse
made from the skin of a little crooked mouse.

It was a long crooked mile back.

THE STRAW

she forgave him his trespasses,
those she knew, and those she guessed at,
so she would have found a way to forgive him
the dark-haired nurse with the coke habit—
same as the others—had it not been
for the day she came home from work
to find them both, smug
with post-coital repleteness
and just-dressedness on her new sofa
that she hadn't even got sitting down on yet herself

ULSTER SAYS NO

Having grown up with so many given negatives
I am always and constitutionally inclined to say yes
yes let's have another drink

yes go on ahead
yes of course you can
yes I'll try that
yes why not?
yes have some of mine
even when it might be more prudent to decline.

THE ART OF TYING FLIES

He's tying a Red Sedge
for those hot summer evenings
or those dead afternoons, July and August,
when he can't quite decide
what to offer the occasional riser,
close under the bank.

The body is hare's ear, spun on orange silk,
and ribbed with gold wire.
Wound all down the body from head to tail,
the hackle comes from a red cockerel.
The wings are Landrail, tied so as to lie
flat along the Sedge's back.
Beeswax the thread, wind and tie,
interweave fur and feather
until they become a living creature again,
reformed, reborn. Finished,

he holds it between his fingers,
lifts it into the light,
sees the graceful wheel of the line
as he lays it down soft as a snowflake

beautiful as any red sedge
fluttering late in the evening sun
on a slow-moving stream.

WORDS FROM THE OTHER SIDE

I visited my friend in hospital,
the day after she had died
and been brought back.
Her heart had stopped, exhausted
by another asthma attack,
by years of pumping
for an easy breath—
kicked back to life only
by doctors and electricity.

The air around her crackled.

Urgently
she pulled me close,
kissed my lips, placed

into the cave of my mouth,
onto my tongue
a message for me, carried back—

death's easy—she said—
much easier than life

and her words hit me
like an amphetamine rush,
dizzied me, left me
electrified, unsure
if I'd been given
a blessing or a curse.

GARY ALLEN

[B. 1959]

BORN AGAIN

Here are the moon children,
hair the colour of barleycorn and bowl-cut round,
quaint neighbours in the townland of Carnalbanagh.

In puzzlement, they stand aloof in the schoolyard
holding hands, like paper dolls in homemade frocks—
their schoolwork always meticulous, if heavy with God.

The Antichrist is real among the broken farm implements,
the shreds of torn dress blowing in the hawthorns—
always at the elbow, he walks with Mass-goers.

In summer they hold baskets of washing for their mother to hang:
and Jacob is a small thing, all day wrestling in the bottom meadow—
the land is full of those who have turned from the Word.

They look at the antics of uncles, aunts, and cousins
with sadness in their large blue eyes,
who balk at grace round the table, unwashed in the blood of the lamb.

God is rather like their father—not to be crossed,
a dry love, silent and exact:
and sometimes at night, this tall house crashes in sin.

TESTAMENT

It was their truth, not mine
though I never questioned what was inbred,
an accepted and natural inevitability—like death.

That they were good men, I had no doubt,
hard-working, sometimes to the exclusion of all else,
yet I was slow to see the fault lines that was contradiction.

My great uncle, a guarded cobbler, mouth full of tacks,
cross-legged at the workshop window,
neither drank nor smoked, yet fathered three illegitimate children.

And my grandfather, whose everyday speech was biblical,
eschewing all that was underhand or false,
dutifully used his blockhammer like an ass's jawbone
on the unemployed Catholics outside the shipyard gate.

Their laws were clear, if not always just,
and need not be spoken to elicit fear,
like Jesus, who hung in every room,
they could see wrongdoing in a child's face.

And God spoke to them, a voice loud as their own,
never to the women, whose bodies harboured sin
(my cousin still bears the strap scars on her back
when he caught her playing with the iron poker).

My grandmother made us kneel and pray
while he was dying in the room above,
then took each of us in turn to pay our last respects.

And although the curtains were drawn on the living world,
with a child's horror I could clearly see
the black blood clotted in each nostril.

At her bidding, I kissed his parchment head
and with fascinated profanity, I whispered
into his cottonwool-plugged ear, Your God is dead.

THE CABINET MAKER

And there you are again, the air thick with dust, the smell of fresh
    cut wood,
shavings curling up your muscular tattooed arms as you cut true —
with the breaker and the iron just right —
the odds and ends of rough planks bartered from the timber yard.

A pot of melted, foul-smelling animal glue on the hearth
and old canvas awnings from the lorry depot covering the floor.

You are lost in these hours as never before
excelling in your strength and discipline,
intuition, skilful fingers, that something in the eye
that taught to tease out the wood, the grain, the precise cut

as you slot dovetail, bevel with a spokeshave and file
and with the small knife you fashioned from the iron in the shipyard

inwardly carve the bone-hard handle for a cabinet door,
consoles for shelves, little catches—
the simple beauty of a drawer with its own whisper and light movement.

BEING

The German shepherd sleeping in the sun
is a stone dog

in my memory:

and I was always awed
by the shafts of light

falling across the disciples
and a serving of simple fare

like the table filling the kitchen,
the tin bath hanging behind the door,

the smell of broth and linseed oil.

For there is meaning in all these things,
or was,

to a lonely child seeking permanence
outside the absence of parents:

a grandfather's roosters,
the withered hand of the old woman in the next yard

reaching through the wire,
caked with excrement.

Then everything changes,
and the moment becomes unsustainable:

on still days
the clack clack of bicycle chain

and the sough of plane over wood
helped me to understand the holding of time,

and the exact perspective of everything.

ON THE FIRST DAY

Those were the days of hunger
long hours stretching like an empty belly

to the tune of the rent-man, club-man, debt-collector.

All my blood were broken to labour,
when labour they could find,

grateful for fifty years of sweat.

And sometimes there was nothing
to chew on, to distract, to hold out for,

each laying blame to the one above.

I took my turn on the wheel:
those eyes old with tiredness,

she gave me the last two cigarettes

and a white breast
that was neither infantile nor sexual

hung useless from the nightdress.

My youth was angry, impotent like the white frost
on the council greens

or the knowledge that my seal was set:

the lorry engines warming up in the depot
seemed to tell me with a sigh,

This is the twenty-eighth world—
and the Lord answered, *The desert among my earths*.

ONE SUMMER EVENING

This woman here
wanted the sun
to make her new,

went out the back
children's ragged clothes
left on the boil,

a husband hammering chairs together
in the front room,

but got no farther
than the line of telegraph poles
stretching like a chain

between peat bogs

and returned disconcerted
to a house where no one knew she had left

and a kitchen steamed
with the loss of light.

THE REVIVAL

All these girls clothed in white—
without a word,
blow down the street
to meet their sisters.

The clouds are high in the sky—
it is summer.

The trains from Belfast
stand at the station
carriage doors flung open.

This way—
my great-grandmother's hand in mine
though I am forty years older—

come down to the river's edge

where Moses waits
a long beard of bulrushes—

a man from Monaghan come up country
having set Dublin in flames.

See how she shines in the water
a child become gold
voices singing free of poverty
bare feet slapping stone.

ANNIVERSARY

These Irish monks wrapped in blankets,
long hair, beards, smelling of rotting flesh
dwell not in mortality
yet subsist on salt and water
though they are distant from any shore:

my uncle was a lay-preacher
spread the word from a wooden gospel hall
carried his bible to work
was abducted as he delivered bread
along the border
and the first emaciated body was laid to rest
with stone and fire:

mutilated before he was shot
three times in the face
his body dumped in a culvert
and booby-trapped with explosives
at the time census forms were soaked
in the blood of a young female worker.

All suffering is real, is complex, is ongoing:
a Dutch girlfriend on the same day, years later,
inadvertently paid in bullets
for a book of poems written in the Maze
while miles away and across a mind-set

the people carried icons
through the streets of West Belfast

and my aunt in a different corner
set the same but yearly changing flowers
on my uncle's grave
and still found faith and forgiveness
in the church none of us could destroy.

CALYPSO

She knows nothing of the outside world
but everything of the heart:

the papery dry fingers clutching the young hand
the odour of eight decades in a floral dress—

come closer, that the faintest of stale breath
on your face gives rise

to the perception of something barely alive.

Fire is her barometer
even when the sun of renewal crosses the threshold
from a street that has moved to the future

her hearth is piled high with cheap grade coal

reflected like the core of a planet
in her stone-wall eyes, giving them sight again.

The dead she knows intimately
has washed a young husband's strong limbs
looked down on the stillborn

identified a son pegged out
on a wasteground of bulldozed houses

each bone crushed to pulp under breezeblocks
the red hole of death in the nape of the neck:

but suffering has formed her
ethereal like the wind in a ship's sails
she fills the livingroom from door to door—

the old heart beating loud as a wrecking-ball.

A DISUSED HOUSE ON THE

BALLYCOWAN ROAD

These old houses fire the imagination
whitewashed gables in the hawthorn hedges
sudden thoughts on narrow roads going nowhere—

who would abandon them?

windows of a doll's house
rafters like the bones of a lost tribe
a garden of nettles and plaster

left to the drifting clouds and wind
the quick flashes of heavy rain—

why were they not levelled altogether?

pegged-out to wither until none can remember
nosing-grounds for dun-covered cows
munching parsley stalks

lapping rust-coloured water from sunken baths.

Oh you crumbling walls of the little counties
none can save you from this slow neglect
here in the green heart of the countryside

penny bridges over dry streams.

And in the pale of the evening
while we settle behind curtains
find no need nor desire to go into the grey estate

I think of the long shadows across the fields
the smell of good earth cooling down
the resilience of our lives, and I'm at peace.

NORTH OF NOWHERE

These are cows that move dumbly
across the gorse and thistles,

but they could be human

alive in their own streams of piss
their inattention to what surrounds them:

in that shed over there I stretched gut
ten hours in salted water

hands ballooning—the bloated maggoty carcass
of one who got too close to the river,

the child who left us to swim the floods.

These beasts are giant
munching the car lights on the motorway
striding the black slated roofs of the housing estate.

Where do cows go to sleep at night mister?
my ma says standing in fields

have you ever seen a bull's balls,

or a pit bull snapping a herd
into the barbed-wire entanglements round the substation,

or the one great staring eye
before the bolt is shot?

I stand outside, covered in shit and blood,
and like a fool I pray.

What are cows used for?
handbags, belts, shoes—

and sometimes, like humans, they look at the moon.

DAMIAN SMYTH

[B. 1962]

TRACKS

The evening he was blown up by his own bomb at the racecourse
he had shaved and showered as though meeting a girlfriend,
Taurus, *Brut* or *Hai Karate* sprinkled like myrrh on his talcy body.

Thrown off the scent, neither family nor friends could track him at
    weekends.
But the bomb that woke the birds and set the hurdles blazing
left his bed in the morning unslept in. There was nothing in the coffin.

Now each Easter, his name is broadcast by loudspeaker over the
    graveyard,
the wind editing the sentences of the tinny oration
that gives out buckets under the silks of flags and emblems.

On the side of the hill, among the tilting headstones, columns of
    marchers
lean as one into the camber of the uneven ground,
the brassy odour of incense drifting like smoke over the shaven heads.

When the breeze brings the tannoy calling the runners and riders miles
    away,
at Binns's big house in the country, where the racecourse
runs for furlongs beside the tarmac road, all you hear is bees.

There is the synchronised swimming of starlings and many trees.

THE ROAD TO NO TOWN

Don't ask me what any of it means
who walked for miles to find the place it named,

turning back, obeying all the rules
of search and recovery, reading all the signs.

Where land is abandoned by the business of farms
and not a sinner left to tell the tale

then those white sheets hanging out to dry
on the hedges are blackthorn blossom.

The clocks of the tarmac tick in the summer sun
                              and all the signposts say

the three Irish miles to go are an each way bet,
though everything's in place just as it should be,

as if—as if somewhere here you'd light on what is real,
the shock of something ordinary and safe

to fix the townland fast to its own grave.
A roadway is threaded through the needle's eye of earth

and follows all the contours your maps show,
its grey old back plunging among the hills

with the certainty of purpose tarmac brings.
But the road to Bright is still the road to no town:

a bearing taken, nothing less than that,
a way not *to* or *from*, but *in* and *through*.

VERONICA

for Martin Lynch

Because they spoiled her view of the lough
from the high stone windows of the fishing lodge,
the cabins on their hunkers down at the water's edge,

the dogs barking and the shouts of children,
wet clothes left out to dry on the whins
and weedy gardens infecting the air,

she sent the land agents in and levelled them,
turning the plots and the sculleries over, ploughing in
the cups and plates, pipe stems and clay jars,

the bits and bobs that couldn't be carried,
breaking up everything human and intact,
bequeathing it all to those engineers, the badgers.

It is hard work despising her. After two hundred years
it takes vigilance, patience and concentration
when there isn't a sign that living was done

underfoot here in the nowhere of Audleystown,
except that in summer that weed veronica
raises its ignorant blue pikes everywhere,

hundreds of them haunting the woods and the hedges,
crowding the pathways, choking the grasses,
                              getting their own back.

BADGERS

Two badgers on the roadside
like drunk old men lain down by a stream.
One dandles its snout in the tarmac,
the other is pressing the long grass flat behind,
its fur abandoned to the wind like smoke.

Afterwards, they'd have slouched to Audleystown,
shouldering their way through hedges and barbed wire,
making dogs bark and the lights go on,
annoying every thing and every one,
padding through the dark, not giving a damn.

When we pulled up beside them for a while,
to be beside them, to watch their native, earthy faces
take the strain of being in the sun,
something of their deaths passed on to us.
The silence of the paths big creatures take,

the surprise of finding their lives next to ours
in unlikely places; their making room for us.

TRANSATLANTIC

The Yanks who touched down at Bishopscourt
came up to Collins's corner along Stream Street,
shuffling in the gutters on each side of the road
in straggly columns of faces almost but not quite our own,
film stars, Harlem Globetrotters, saxophone players,

exactly as they staggered in Market Street
across the screen in the Grand, lounging through a war:
Bronx wit, Jewish noses, brash, different and liked;
a homeboy army occupying the quiet lives of Down
turning up in talk for years, like ghosts or eccentrics,

occasions for encounters where locals got the upper hand:
'Mind them big blacks on the road? Them's the boys.'

And, decades after, when refugees from Lenadoon and Hannastown
strung their dramatic wagon trains to the Flying Horse Estate,
the old Norman parishes of Ballyhornan and Inch

bracing themselves once more to be billeted on,
the 'international peace-keeping force' still meant Americans,
bloody from Cambodia and Ho Chi Minh. But it was the English,
encamped as always at Ballykinler and turned out like clergy,
their boots munching the tarmac almost, but not quite, like applause,

who rolled out the bales of barbed wire like brushwood. The English
familiar, predictable and unremarkable, exactly like us.

GHOSTS

Although the mourners at the funeral in Raholp
fell in behind his coffin at the gate,
the dead man from his bedroom still peeped out,
the blue wound like a feather in his scalp.

How can such things be in these strange days
when every townland, cautious of its dead,
disciplines the corpses to be sad
and not disturb the curate while he prays?

Now there are so many in the news,
the dead should travel silently to ground
by whatever means the headlines understand
and not set out to frighten or amuse.

SKEFFINGTONS

Or *Skivvitons*, as our own talking had it,
the ospidal, antiticks, turmits, loo-warm tea,
step-leathers, grewhouns and the vit,
a universe took shape with every estimate.

These words were like jerkins worn inside out:
still working for their keep and doing well,
with scars and stitches, nips and tucks,
swapping the big world's pattern for their own.

PADDY CELTIC

My brother kicked points for Downpatrick
by just standing over the ball and drawing his boot back:
no ritual, no run up, the ball between the posts.
The umpires, my father said, would reach for their wee flags

as soon as Paddy Celtic placed the ball.
And so he passed into legend in his own town
like Oisín, doing feats of local loyalty,
throwing baskets for the *Ardglass Sharks,*

clearing soldiers from the Portofino Cafe,
being sound, outrageous and reliable,
a holy terror when angry, drunk when drunk,
knowing my father well and loving him.

My father in the heart ward. My brother, old beside the bed,
watching the laces of blood tying the old man to machines.
In the washing, thirty years ago, a boxing vest soaked in blood.
'Soaked in blood,' he said, 'and none of it me own.'

DISAPPEARED

Along the border, where x marks the spot,
the bodies have moulted from the black bin bags
that did them as shrouds in the hurry of night.

Now at Rossglass the seals break the surface,
the souls of the dead peering sadly ashore,
balaclavas of pelt pulled tight on their skulls.

FROM CEMETERY SUNDAY

I

On Cemetery Sunday,
I took the top grave:
in the children's quarter,
no markers, no marble,

a half acre limbo of lumpy ground.
Backed up to the wall
by the old road to Killough,
at the only headstone,

John Linton lay down,
the tenant of the highest point
on a hillside of dead,
all County Down stretched out round him.

To my father at the middle grave
and my brothers at the bottom
was the small matter of a hundred years.
His grandmother, uncles and his father

had each laid down whole lives beneath our feet.
Still between the brackets of one century
a dozen fragile lives proliferate.

II

Unlike the Maxwells, Bretts, Southwells and the Fordes,
the poor have little history in a place.
To have their corpses handy to the door,
they'd move the sick in the Workhouse to the ground floor
so the cart that brought the oats in from the town
could carry their bodies out to unmarked graves
in two acres of lumpy ground on the Strangford Road.

There certainly is a tale of the cathedral singing,
Dickensian cabinet-makers, of aprons and top hats
and daffodils in spring round the family vaults,
the solidity of monuments; but I can't clear my head
of the fog of holocaust beneath that gentleness,
the dead piled up like turf against the wall,
the Asylum's invisible graveyard at the Model Farm Estate.

VI

My great-grandmother's Lodging House
at the top of the Shambles in John Street,
took in those travellers on their way through
the City of Down to the coast, or inland
to the richer pastures from off the boats.
On the very site, where the roads still break

to Ardglass and Killough on left and right,
the Hospital of St John of the English

spread with the Leper House of St Nicholas
low buildings out along the hill, their orchards
and cells staring across the flooded valley
to Patrick, Brigid and Columcille

whose bones are thrust like the roots of trees
into the sanctuary of God's earth,
one crowded grave for the three of them
under the Cathedral's plain square haunches.
In the end, where those bodies are
is neither here nor there; not to have

the good fortune of headstones
is not unusual enough to remark upon
in the City of Down or the Barony of Lecale
or the massive parish that passes for Ulster
where a signpost will point far off to the townland
whose boundaries you are within already

and the dead turn up where they're least expected,
in school playgrounds; or are lost forever
below grid references no one can remember.
The Hospital of St John of the English,
by right and charter from the conquest of Ireland,
could seize itself of a certain custom

whereby the Prior could dip his tureen
for two large measures (of uncertain amount)
in every brewing of ale in the City.

Here, Mr Trotter in 1728
'*making a new garden on Chappel Hill …*
found vast quantities of human bones
which he deposited in one large grave'.

VII

John Linton's son lies in Rawalpindi
in the colours of the Inniskilling Fusiliers

and Henry Smyth's at Ladysmith
and Bernard, underground in Barrow-in-Furness,

is my father's twin in the scarf and flat cap
he's wearing for the camera in 1918,

the year the mine collapses on him,
nine years before my father's born.

I know these people. Their faces are mine
and I take my place by the vacant graves

because the bones of your people count
and because the shadows of their features pass

across your own down a hundred years
and happiness and heartbreak simply count.

They swarm like bees to the honey of blood,
mustering like demobbed infantry in the yard

and each bangs in turn on my scullery door
to be let inside, to be out of the cold:

Warren Stranney, Mary Owens, Edward Potter, Tommy John,
McGrorys, Connollys, McKeevers, Galbraiths,
Irvines, McKennas, Lavertys, Lennons, Kellys,
and all of the people who passed through the Lodging House,

and all of the clergy who served in the Parish,
and all of those who died in the Troubles

Those souls I never knew and have forgotten.

FROM THE DOWN RECORDER

My father's prayer book's fat with memoriam cards,
hundreds of dead, their faces bleached but living,
photographs picked and cut from family snaps,
outings, weddings, christenings, or else

an accidental capture by the by.
They are stacked in a catacomb of prayer.

Pages so fragile they might let ink slip through
contain them perfectly. They are so at home,

strangers to each other and themselves.
Across the townlands their images reflect
on homes they rarely visited, if ever, on friends
whose skins they touched but fleetingly

and on whose careful watch their souls depend.
Hundreds of dead. Hundreds gone to seed
the same earth that will, tomorrow or today,
fall open at the right place, like a book.

ANDY WHITE

[B. 1962]

THE STREET SYMPHONY OF NAPOLI

If I could write
the street symphony
of Napoli
it would start with you walking into
that Italian bar
if I could write
the street symphony of Napoli
it would be played by a
thousand ruined cars

dilapidated
beyond repair
their horns blaring

never in time
never in tune
and the score would be
stolen from my hotel room

HEY MAN, THERE'S AN ULSTER POET

IN THE HOTEL LOBBY

Ulster poet
seated
on location
on commission
slim volumes
thing past

Suddenly
Cuchulain and his
axe
swing into Reception
lights up a Gallaher's blue
the poet fondles his
pen
'Leave me alone' shouts Cuch
'I'm immortalised already
Give me peace
whoojoo think y'are
Louis Macfuckingneice?
Don't drag me into a poem
I'm averse to it.'

Outside in the street
bit of bother
people hurling
anthologies at each other

ONE

The government of love
has increased its majority
by one

Christine holding on
and pushing out

and now
Sebastian
is lying serious beside her

and the government of love
has increased its majority
by one

THE DICTATORSHIP OF RHYME

It happens all the time

ROAD TO ZILINA

Willie Nelson singing
on the road again
on the radio
headed for Zilina

chimneys and funnels
and cranes and concrete
and concrete and cranes
and snow-capped mountains
above the dead trees
of the dying forest

THE COUNTRY OF DIVIS FLATS

Imagine a country where
everybody
lives in Divis flats
because this is Eastern Europe
and you can't turn the corner
for a more respectable view

the grey grim distances
of towerblock balconies

in the driven acid rain
sad factories
still standing in yellow smoke
while farmers ride carts stamped
17th century
toothless old women
struggle for bread
with empty shopping bags and
the young pray
that this time can belong to them

communism is a crashed Skoda
on the cracked highway
beyond repair
exhaust still running

what do we fight for?
while we have food and
clothes and clean air
imagine a country where
everyone lives
in Divis flats
for ever
and imagine a country
where the killing could stop
tomorrow

NIGHT FALLS ON VIENNA

River right through
this city
low tide at night
young lovers sit
have a cigarette and
pass their time
as the birds curl up on
the statues of an empire
long gone
night falls on
Vienna

tourist buses park on the
city limits
opera house opens its door
sausage stands sell
beer
near the sculpted subway
the one down and out
in old Vienna
twitches
like he's in Central Park
as night falls on
Vienna

the smog meter
on the cathedral wall
reads zero
and the cocktail crowds waltz
to celebrate
nothing in particular
and the world cannot hold
so many
beautiful women

dawn's first flicker
touches the sky with grey
the ornate carvings still
stand still
the lovers tuck up
together
the beautiful women meet
their beautiful Viennese beds
the empire survives another evening
night has fallen
on Vienna

HALLE

The town that man forgot
to clean

BREAD ROLL

Opened an Austrian roll
smelled the soft
dough inside
felt like Proust

on holiday in the
Tyrol
a morning
a mother's kiss

AIRBORNE IN WARTIME

1

There is
no war
in the
Dublin Evening Herald
just gossip about a girl
and a picture of
the world's biggest matchstick

2

Mont Blanc
from Swissair
neutral at 3000 ft
shivers up my spine
sun hit the snow
in perfect time
as we
descended to Geneva

why
when the errand boys of
America and Iraq
made this same descent
did they not look left to
Mont Blanc and see
the white surrender flag
of God's big world
and realise
how low they crawled
on this earth
and the high necessity
not to curse this world
with their dirty
little
war

3

There's a rim of
fire on the
horizon curve of the earth
this evening

before taking off
Aer Lingus
neutral ground level
I heard all the leaders
saying no in different languages

tonight's the night
the war should stop
the oil wells are burning and
down there
is too far to drop
into the
man-made sunset

PALE DRIVER

Death
rides a pale tank
skull and gaping eyes

and the forces' sweetheart
on the turret
hitching up her skirt

the end is over the
horizon
just an extra mile
and the pale apocalypse tank-driver
shakes his head to smile
he knows the other three
aren't that far behind

PIPES OVER ARDOYNE

There are no
For Sale signs
and no shopfronts
just carryout bags
and modern kids in
modern rags
colours garish
against the grey

there's a low level storm
general over Belfast
helicopter skies

and like the bar that
never stops serving
there's pipes over Ardoyne
tonight

finished
7 in the morning
and the closed circuit
black & white
shows you daylight before
you emerge
no signs
no shopfronts
but the carryout bags
and the stragglers
and the wee boys by the burger van
are struggling
with the fact of
the morning

the litter's in drifts
like autumn in August
we felt the lift
and the fall
of pipes over Ardoyne

AT THE FORTY FOOT, 4 A.M.

The fear
of seeing your
abandoned clothes
at the forty foot
deep moonlit sea
no sign of your
skinny dipped body

only the lapping of
the water
the lighthouses
answering each other
across the bay
and your
abandoned clothes

I felt the fear
in my love
as the tower was
silhouetted against
scattering clouds
and a poetry moon hung
unbearable cold
over the forty foot

and you were
unreachable
naked

I always hated swimming
and she so brave
4 a.m.
at the forty foot

YELLOW TEAPOT OF THE WORLD

Lime Street in November
clear cold and bright
she'd sneaked into the hotel by the back stairs
the night before

we stepped out
two pounds in our pockets
and everything was OK
like it is sometimes

that Liverpool morning we bought
the yellow teapot of the world
because it was ours to buy
that morning

CLASSIC POEMS

CIARAN CARSON

[B. 1948]

EESTI

I wandered homesick-lonely through that Saturday of silent Tallinn
When a carillon impinged a thousand raining quavers on my ear,
   tumbling

Dimly from immeasurable heights into imaginary brazen gong-space,
   trembling
Dimpled in their puddled, rain-drop halo-pools, concentrically
   assembling.

I glimpsed the far-off, weeping onion-domes. I was inveigled towards
   the church
Through an aural labyrinth of streets until I sheltered in its porch.

I thumbed the warm brass worn thumb-scoop of the latch. *Tock.*
   I entered into bronze —
Dark, shrines and niches lit by beeswax tapers and the sheen of ikons.

Their eyes and the holes in their hands were nailed into my gaze, *quod*
   erat domonstrandum·

Digits poised and pointed towards their hearts. They are beautiful
    Panjandrums

Invoked by murmuring and incense, hymns that father passes on to
    father,
The patina of faces under painted faces. They evoke another

Time, where I am going with you, father, to first Mass. We walked
The starry frozen pavement, holding hands to stop ourselves from
    falling. There was no talk,

Nor need for it. Our incense-breath was word enough as we approached
    the Gothic,
Shivering in top-coats, on the verge of sliding off the metronomic

Azure-gradual dawn as nave and transept summoned us with beaded,
    thumbed
And fingered whispering. Silk-tasselled missals. Rosaries. Statues
    stricken dumb

Beneath their rustling purple shrouds, as candles wavered in the holy
    smoke.
The mosaic chapel echoed with a clinking, chinking censer-music.

This red-letter day would not be written, had I not wandered through
    the land of Eesti.
I asked my father how he thought it went. He said to me in Irish, *Listen:
    Éist.*

BELFAST CONFETTI

Suddenly as the riot squad moved in, it was raining exclamation marks,
Nuts, bolts, nails, car-keys. A fount of broken type. And the explosion
Itself—an asterisk on the map. This hyphenated line, a burst of rapid
    fire . . .
I was trying to complete a sentence in my head, but it kept stuttering,
All the alleyways and side-streets blocked with stops and colons.

I know this labyrinth so well—Balaclava, Raglan, Inkerman, Odessa
    Street—
Why can't I escape? Every move is punctuated. Crimea Street. Dead
    end again.
A Saracen, Kremlin-2 mesh. Makrolon face-shields. Walkie-talkies.
    What is
My name? Where am I coming from? Where am I going? A fusillade of
    question-marks.

THE IRISH FOR NO

Was it a vision, or a waking dream? I heard her voice before I saw
What looked like the balcony scene in *Romeo and Juliet*, except Romeo
Seemed to have shinned up a pipe and was inside arguing with her.
    The casements
Were wide open and I could see some Japanese-style wall-hangings, the
    dangling

Quotation marks of a yin-yang mobile. *It's got nothing*, she was snarling,
    nothing
To do with politics, and, before the bamboo curtain came down,
That goes for you too!

It was time to turn into the dog's-leg short-cut from Chlorine Gardens
Into Cloreen Park, where you might see an *Ulster Says No* scrawled on
    the side
Of the power-block—which immediately reminds me of the Eglantine
    Inn
Just on the corner: on the missing *h* of Cloreen, you might say. We were
    debating,
Bacchus and the pards and me, how to render *The Ulster Bank—*
    the Bank
That Likes to Say Yes into Irish, and whether eglantine was alien to Ireland.
I cannot see what flowers are at my feet, when *yes* is the verb repeated,
Not exactly yes, but phatic nods and whispers. *The Bank That Answers All*
Your Questions, maybe? That Greek portico of Mourne granite, dazzling
With promises and feldspar, mirrors you in the Delphic black of its
    windows.

And the bruised pansies of the funeral parlour are dying in reversed gold
    letters,
The long sigh of the afternoon is not yet complete on the promontory
    where the victim,
A corporal in the UDR from Lisbellaw, was last seen having driven over
    half
Of Ulster, a legally-held gun was found and the incidence of stress
    came up

On the headland which shadows Larne Harbour and the black pitch of
    warehouses.
There is a melancholy blast of diesel, a puff of smoke which might be
    black or white.
So the harbour slips away to perilous seas as things remain unsolved;
    we listen
To the *ex cathedra* of the fog-horn, and *drink and leave the world
    unseen —*

What's all this to the Belfast business-man who drilled
Thirteen holes in his head with a Black & Decker? It was just a normal
    morning
When they came. The tennis-court shone with dew or frost, a little
    before dawn.
The border, it seemed, was not yet crossed: the Milky Way trailed snowy
    brambles,
The stars clustered thick as blackberries. They opened the door into the
    dark:
The murmurous haunt of flies on summer eves. Empty jam-jars.
Mish-mash. Hotch-potch. And now you rub your eyes and get
    acquainted with the light
A dust of something reminiscent drowses over the garage smell of
    creosote,
The concrete: blue clouds in porcelain, a paint-brush steeped in a
    chipped cup;
Staples hyphenate a wet cardboard box as the upturned can of oil still
    spills
And the unfed cat toys with the yin yang of a tennis-ball, debating
    whether *yes* is *no*.

MEDBH MCGUCKIAN

[B. 1950]

TULIPS

Touching the tulips was a shyness
I had had for a long time—such
Defensive mechanisms to frustrate the rain
That shakes into the sherry glass
Of the daffodil, though scarcely
Love's young dream; such present-mindedness
To double-lock in tiers as whistle-tight,
Or catch up on sleep with cantilevered
Palms cupping elbows. It's their independence
Tempts them to this grocery of soul.

Except, like all governesses, easily
Carried away, in sunny
Absences of mirrors they exalt themselves
To ballets of revenge, a kind
Of twinness, an olympic way of earning,
And are sacrificed to plot, their faces
Lifted many times to the artistry of light—

Its lovelessness a deeper sort
Of illness than the womanliness
Of tulips with their bee-dark hearts.

THE FLITTING

'You wouldn't believe all this house has cost me—
In body-language terms, it has turned me upside down.'
I've been carried from one structure to the other
On a chair of human arms, and liked the feel
Of being weightless, that fraternity of clothes …
Now my own life hits me in the throat, the bumps
And cuts of the walls as telling
As the poreholes in strawberries, tomato seeds.
I cover them for safety with these Dutch girls
Making lace, or leaning their almond faces
On their fingers with a mandolin, a dreamy
Chapelled ease abreast this other turquoise-turbanned,
Glancing over her shoulder with parted mouth.

She seems a garden escape in her unconscious
Solidarity with darkness, clove-scented
As an orchid taking fifteen years to bloom,
And turning clockwise as the honeysuckle.
Who knows what importance
She attaches to the hours?

Her narrative secretes its own values, as mine might
If I painted the half of me that welcomes death
In a faggoted dress, in a peacock chair,
No falser biography than our casual talk
Of losing a virginity, or taking a life, and
No less poignant if dying
Should consist in more than waiting.

I postpone my immortality for my children,
Little rock-roses, cushioned
In long-flowering sea-thrift and metrics,
Lacking elemental memories:
I am well-earthed here as the digital clock,
Its numbers flicking into place like overgrown farthings
On a bank where once a train
Ploughed like an emperor living out a myth
Through the cambered flesh of clover and wild carrot.

ON BALLYCASTLE BEACH

If I found you wandering round the edge
Of a French-born sea, when children
Should be taken in by their parents,
I would read these words to you,
Like a ship coming in to harbour,
As meaningless and full of meaning

As the homeless flow of life
From room to homesick room.

The words and you would fall asleep,
Sheltering just beyond my reach
In a city that has vanished to regain
Its language. My words are traps
Through which you pick your way
From a damp March to an April date,
Or a mid-August misstep; until enough winter
Makes you throw your watch, the heartbeat
Of everyone present, out into the snow.

My forbidden squares and your small circles
Were a book that formed within you
In some pocket, so permanently distended,
That what does not face north, faces east.
Your hand, dark as a cedar lane by nature,
Grows more and more tired of the skidding light,
The hunched-up waves, and all the wet clothing,
Toys and treasures of a late summer house.

Even the Atlantic has begun its breakdown
Like a heavy mask thinned out scene after scene
In a more protected time — like one who has
Gradually, unnoticed, lengthened her pre-wedding
Dress. But, staring at the old escape and release
Of the water's speech, faithless to the end,
Your voice was the longest I heard in my mind,
Although I had forgotten there could be such light.

PAUL MULDOON

[B. 1951]

IRELAND

The Volkswagen parked in the gap,
But gently ticking over.
You wonder if it's lovers
And not men hurrying back
Across two fields and a river.

HISTORY

Where and when exactly did we first have sex?
Do you remember? Was it Fitzroy Avenue,
Or Cromwell Road, or Notting Hill?
Your place or mine? Marseilles or Aix?
Or as long ago as that Thursday evening
When you and I climbed through the bay window
On the ground floor of Aquinas Hall
And into the room where MacNeice wrote 'Snow',
Or the room where they say he wrote 'Snow'?

HAY

This much I know. Just as I'm about to make that right turn
off Province Line Road
I meet another beat-up Volvo
carrying a load

of hay. (More accurately, a bale of lucerne
on the roof rack,
a bale of lucerne or fescue or alfalfa.)
My hands are raw. I'm itching to cut the twine, to unpack

that hay-accordion, that hay-concertina.
It must be ten o'clock. There's still enough light
(not least from the glow

of the bales themselves) for a body to ascertain
that when one bursts, as now, something takes flight
from those hot and heavy box-pleats. This much, at least, I know.

FROM INCANTATA

in memory of Mary Farl Powers

I thought of you tonight, *a leanbh*, lying there in your long barrow
colder and dumber than a fish by Francisco de Herrera,

as I X-Actoed from a spud the Inca
glyph for a mouth: thought of that first time I saw your pink
spotted torso, distant-near as a nautilus,
when you undid your portfolio, yes indeedy,
and held the print of what looked like a cankered potato
at arm's length—your arms being longer, it seemed, than Lugh's.

Even Lugh of the Long (sometimes the Silver) Arm
would have wanted some distance between himself and the army-worms
that so clouded the sky over St Cloud you'd have to seal
the doors and windows and steel
yourself against their nightmarish *déjeuner sur l'herbe*:
try as you might to run a foil
across their tracks, it was to no avail;
the army-worms shinnied down the stove-pipe on an army-worm rope.

I can hardly believe that, when we met, my idea of 'R and R'
was to get smashed, almost every night, on sickly-sweet Demerara
rum and Coke: as well as leaving you a grass widow
(remember how Krapp looks up 'viduity'?),
after eight or ten or twelve of those dark rums
it might be eight or ten or twelve o'clock before I'd land
back home in Landseer Street, deaf and blind
to the fact that not only was I all at sea, but in the doldrums.

Again and again you'd hold forth on your own version of Thomism,
your own *Summa*
Theologiae that in everything there is an order,
that the things of the world sing out in a great oratorio:

it was Thomism, though, tempered by *La Nausée*,
by His Nibs Sam Bethicket,
and by that Dublin thing, that an artist must walk down Baggott
Street wearing a hair-shirt under the shirt of Nessus.

'*D'éirigh me ar maidin*,' I sang, '*a tharraingt chun aoinigh mhóir*':
our first night, you just had to let slip that your secret amour
for a friend of mine was such
that you'd end up lying with him in a ditch
under a bit of whin, or gorse, or furze,
somewhere on the border of Leitrim, perhaps, or Roscommon:
'gamine,' I wanted to say, 'kimono';
even then it was clear I'd never be at the centre of your universe.

Nor should I have been, since you were there already, your own *Ding
an sich*, no less likely to take wing
than the Christ you drew for a Christmas card as a pupa
in swaddling clothes: and how resolutely you would pooh pooh
the idea I shared with Vladimir and Estragon,
with whom I'd been having a couple of jars,
that this image of the Christ-child swaddled and laid in the manger
could be traced directly to those army-worm dragoons.

I thought of the night Vladimir was explaining to all and sundry
the difference between *geantrai* and *suantrai*
and you remarked on how you used to have a crush
on Burt Lancaster as Elmer Gantry, and Vladimir went to brush
the ash off his sleeve with a legerdemain
that meant only one thing—'Why does he put up with this crap?'—

and you weighed in with 'To live in a dustbin, eating scrap,
seemed to Nagg and Nell a most eminent domain.'

How little you were exercised by those tiresome literary intrigues,
how you urged me to have no more truck
than the Thane of Calder
with a fourth estate that professes itself to be '*égalitaire*'
but wants only blood on the sand: yet, irony of ironies,
you were the one who, in the end,
got yourself up as a *retiarius* and, armed with net and trident,
marched from Mount Street to the Merrion Square arena.

In the end, you were the one who went forth to beard the lion,
you who took the DART line
every day from Jane's flat in Dun Laoghaire, or Dalkey,
dreaming your dream that the subterranean Dodder and Tolka
might again be heard above the *hoi polloi*
for whom Irish 'art' means a High Cross at Carndonagh or Corofin
and *The Book of Kells*: not until the lion cried craven
would the poor Tolka and the poor Dodder again sing out for joy.

I saw you again tonight, in your jump-suit, thin as a rake,
your hand moving in such a deliberate arc
as you ground a lithographic stone
that your hand and the stone blurred to one
and your face blurred into the face of your mother, Betty Wahl,
who took your failing, ink-stained hand
in her failing, ink-stained hand
and together you ground down that stone by sheer force of will.

I remember your pooh poohing, as we sat there on the 'Enterprise',
my theory that if your name is Powers
you grow into it or, at least,
are less inclined to tremble before the likes of this bomb-blast
further up the track: I myself was shaking like a leaf
as we wondered whether the I.R.A. or the Red
Hand Commandos or even the Red
Brigades had brought us to a standstill worthy of Hamm and Clov.

Hamm and Clov; Nagg and Nell; Watt and Knott;
the fact is that we'd been at a standstill long before the night
things came to a head,
long before we'd sat for half the day in the sweltering heat
somewhere just south of Killnasaggart
and I let slip a name—her name—off my tongue
and you turned away (I see it now) the better to deliver the sting
in your own tail, to let slip your own little secret.

I thought of you again tonight, thin as a rake, as you bent
over the copper plate of 'Emblements',
its tidal wave of army-worms into which you all but disappeared:
I wanted to catch something of its spirit
and yours, to body out your disembodied *vox*
clamantis in deserto, to let this all-too-cumbersome device
of a potato-mouth in a potato-face
speak out, unencumbered, from its long, low, mould-filled box.

I wanted it to speak to what seems always true of the truly great,
that you had a winningly inaccurate

sense of your own worth, that you would second-guess
yourself too readily by far, that you would rally to any cause
before your own, mine even,
though you detected in me a tendency to put
on too much artificiality, both as man and poet,
which is why you called me 'Polyester' or 'Polyurethane'.

That last time in Dublin, I copied with a quill dipped in oak-gall
onto a sheet of vellum, or maybe a human caul,
a poem for *The Great Book of Ireland*: as I watched the low
swoop over the lawn today of a swallow
I thought of your animated talk of Camille Pissarro
and André Derain's *The Turning Road, L'Estaque*:
when I saw in that swallow's nest a face in a mud-pack
from that muddy road I was filled again with a profound sorrow.

You must have known already, as we moved from the 'Hurly Burly'
to McDaid's or Riley's,
that something was amiss: I think you even mentioned a homeopath
as you showed off the great new acid-bath
in the Graphic Studio, and again undid your portfolio
to lay out your latest works; I try to imagine the strain
you must have been under, pretending to be as right as rain
while hearing the bells of a church from some long-flooded valley.

From the Quabbin reservoir, maybe, where the banks and bakeries
of a dozen little submerged Pompeii reliquaries
still do a roaring trade: as clearly as I saw your death-mask
in that swallow's nest, you must have heard the music

rise from the muddy ground between
your breasts as a nocturne, maybe, by John Field;
to think that you thought yourself so invulnerable, so inviolate,
that a little cancer could be beaten.

You must have known, as we walked through the ankle-deep clabber
with Katherine and Jean and the long-winded Quintus Calaber,
that cancer had already made such a breach
that you would almost surely perish:
you must have thought, as we walked through the woods
along the edge of the Quabbin,
that rather than let some doctor cut you open
you'd rely on infusions of hardock, hemlock, all the idle weeds.

I thought again of how art may be made, as it was by André Derain,
of nothing more than a turn
in the road where a swallow dips into the mire
or plucks a strand of bloody wool from a strand of barbed wire
in the aftermath of Chickamauga or Culloden
and builds from pain, from misery, from a deep-seated hurt,
a monument to the human heart
that shines like a golden dome among roofs rain-glazed and leaden . . .

MATT KIRKHAM

[B. 1966]

THE MUSEUM OF TRANSPORT

Many stories start with a journey:
the sea's weighing up our dhow,
or junk, or clipper, and canvas claps
against the mast as we're told of mainsails,
hawsers, spinnakers. Or what we hear
is the grate and cough and rush
as coke is shovelled into the boiler.
We sense pressure in the intimate gauges
and know the tracks are singing
or the tyres are singing as the motorway
shifts into concrete. Landscape is liquid
and we cannot stop passing through it.

This is the place our journeying has taken us,
where we are in unceasing motion.
Within our walls, we've made them exhibits,
abandoned them to their stillnesses,
to orbit them, as we might the stars,
untouchable.

THE MUSEUM OF TRASH

You may be able to reconstruct
lost communities from clay pipes, hog-gut
condoms, a baked-earth thumbpiece of pot handle,
broken-nibbed quills,

but will they resurrect this museum,
re-site it on a future landfill,
given an outsized greywhite feather from the costume
of your tour guide, Sammy Seagull,

or the torn ticket stubs,
iced lolly wrappers, Snickers wrappers, cigarette butts
the ripped boxes that held
those Matchbox toy dustcarts we sell?

THE MUSEUM OF THE AFTERLIFE

Nirvana was tough. For Valhalla, the axes
were sent by the Viking Museum. Hell's furnaces
we salvaged from the Steelworks Heritage Park;
found in a municipal museum's yard,
the clear fountains plashing in Islam's paradise.
Our guidebook's *The Book of the Dead*. When Anubis

weighs your heart he employs a set of brass panscales
reclaimed from the Folk Park's grocer's, and yes, we stole
without consequence his Feather of Truth, a very
rare goose feather, from the Rare Breeds Open Farm. Our ferry
they'd no space for at the Lifeboat Museum. In the end,
a featureless white room, an installation sent
by the Museum of Abstraction, provided
us with our Nirvana. I'm Virgil. I'll be your guide.

THE MUSEUM OF EXTINCT SPECIES

I'll plait your hair
into a brunette ammonite.

I'll fashion a brooch
from the fritillary and its pin,

polish the iguanodon claw,
drill through it with an antler,

thread it on a strip of aurochs hide,
a pendant for your neck

I can't escape, yes,
comparing to ivory,

In every direction the museum,
my love, stretches a city mile.

Each morning
we wait for the jewels of the day.

A BLUE BIRO FROM THE

MUSEUM OF CALLIGRAPHY

It's been on the point of dying out
for three millennia. Since they stopped
using hieroglyphs. Since they stopped sending
letters. Cross the 'hieroglyphs', write 'the quill'.
From the death of the scroll. Since the fire
in the Library of Alexandria.
Since universal education opened it
to the children of the menial classes.
Cross out 'the quill'. Write in 'vellum'.

What is stopping you from writing your postcards
with your Museum of Calligraphy
blue biro is the way the waves keep lifting
the giraffe-skin pattern of sunlight
they themselves form on the floor of the sandy
shallows, and projecting it up the beach

towards your lounger, then withdrawing,
taking it back, retracting hissingly,
and there, the pattern is there again.

Since the invention of the blue biro.
Cross out 'the blue biro', write in 'e-mail'.
Being on the point of dying out
makes it a tragic artform, like postcards
or the local currency, or not speaking
English stroke American. Cross out
'tragic', write 'nostalgic'. Cross out 'e-mail',
write 'textphone'. Cross out 'nostalgic', write 'hidebound'.
Cross out 'hidebound', write 'nostalgic'.

THE MUSEUM OF CENSORSHIP

For black and white figures, before and after
they were airbrushed from their black and white photos,
we are keeping this gallery of spaces.

We are keeping this for the dust
from a statue of the Buddha, or maybe
for a woman's face. To be a curator
you must be inspired by the beauty
of pieces that emphasise what is lost.

Though emphasise is wrong. For phalluses
chipped from Hindu or Egyptian statues—
look elsewhere for the statues themselves—
we are keeping this gallery of spaces.

We are in a cathedral after the civil war,
counting our places, in the absence of saints.

A MUSEUM IN NEGATIVE

In the way a picture of Myra Hindley
made out of children's handprints
is the negative of the Museum of Childhood

and in the way the white Arctic
that makes sense of the Inuit's ash
and walrus-gut or walrus-hide snowshoe
is the negative of the black page,
alas, poor Yorick, from *Tristram
Shandy*, itself a hole lifted
from a play about a Dane, which,
as a creature made from body parts,
I assert my right to insert,

and in the way the stacked spectacles
at Auschwitz and the names
in the Holocaust Museum

are the negative of
a famous Hollywood face's
collection of Nazi memorabilia

when I assert that my writing her
puts her on show, in a museum,

a Monster, a freak, and my
looking her in the eye
and knowing she looks back with a human eye
like mine shows my humanity,

she, Mary, says that what makes
a monster is this asserting
that this is human, this is not, this is.

JOHN STONE

I swear. The dance of his mouth and tongue,
the lad hanged for striking down the doc,
these I've not carved, nor that abbot's rolling lip,
shredding some lad's cassock with his eyes.

Nor three teeth in my grandmother's gob
as she told my father there'd been work for his father,
and would be life's work for him and for his son.
And old John the Stonecarver my father's father died,

and so my granddame threetooth died.
It was not chipped out by my chisel, by my hand.
But they raised us up, sons of men,
our mallets and blades, by hoists and by ladders,

after the abbot's boy grassed. His phizzog,
his leer a gargoyle. We swung higher
than grindstone's grate and whine on metal,
and they tell us the pit is split by screams,

but I see again his chisel, his mallet
descending beside his tumble into silence,
freed of his forsaking hand, my father's,
carving that declining and final air between us.

And gathered then their gawking turned to me,
high heavenwards. Now I am John Stone.
By this ale in this hand I will tell what in a stone
finds the face of a devil, what a saint's.

THE NATIONAL PAINT GALLERY

Tell me, with Taurus your Dad's birth sign
and your mother born on Good Friday,
why shouldn't we label each exhibit
with the chemical formula of the paint?

Hang each artist's palette by their canvas?
Why are the gift shop's walls in zesty yellow?

Who's been daubing sloeberry juice and soot,
red clay and piss on your cave's walls?
What made the skyblue of the skies
above the cornflowers in your father's father's meadow,
through the attic window of your mother's mother's house
the summer days your parents were conceived?

IN THE TEA MUSEUM

Before she slipped her peachblossom sash
through your nosering, you wouldn't be led.
You'd brewed up a storm from dried shit and straw,
clattering down the ramp through the stumbling yells
of the abattoir lads. Wasn't it frosty
beneath your hooves, the lobby's marble floor?

Before she guided you by her right little finger
back through the wreckage, her left hand
clasping her loosened gown over, you'd been the kind
to rush at your two-horned reflection, shattering
display cases, acting out ambiguities,
dragon or charger, lion or unicorn.
But weren't your imaginary matadors

just panicked visitors, dropping
their freetrade Earl Grey for you to stamp on?

Before your all-black and glassy eyes
took in her porcelain face, you'd shown
no discrimination. You'd trampled Wedgwood
and novelty teapots in Hollywood faces.
Chests of Assam and Lapsang Souchong
you'd splintered, and the model clipper,
the racket sending the kimono'd girls
scurrying from their ceremonies, one two three,
your bull ears cocked at the stories whispered
in the tiny paired pattering of their size fours.
Didn't security, stirred from his cuppa,
lock you in before they could find the last geisha?

After the debris settled, as you stood four-hooved and still,
the CD of that bamboo flute still playing somewhere,
before she'd made a left-horned unicorn of you,
the last unbroken teapot gently rocking,
blue-white, on your right horn, you highstepping after,
gingerly, where china had lodged in your hooves,
hadn't she held the steaming cup to your nostrils
with its peachflower scents and its underscents
of soil turned beneath Himalayan foothills,
earth where your hoofprints are holy?

THE CIRCULAR MUSEUM

You set down your cup and saucer and doughnut and check your watch. The second hand is just nodding past its zenith. Sitting in the courtyard on the low circular wall—this stonework could be the missing chunks from the seventeenth-century mill stone, from the Mayan calendar stone—that bounds the pond, you watch the wavelets expand from the fountain, at first smaller than the Victorian wedding ring but soon the size of the museum's CD ROM, that Celtic torque, now the wet diameter of the cannonball from the Mary Rose, and as they grow the ripples cut into each other, cross-weaving their shadows on the pool's mosaic floor, momentarily cancelling each other only to reappear, reinforced, now rolling smoothly, larger than the diameter of the Roman chariot wheel laid flat, the steam age train wheels, perfect as the tinny and glinting curl on that Coke ringpull you passed to the blonde girl back in that playground marriage, as the smoothness of your ring finger's skin now when the ring slips up, down. A gentle pulse has emerged from the fountain's chaos, licking at the wall where you sit. You take a sip from your teacup. The sun is no longer making patterns on the pond's floor. Soon it will even sink behind the museum building—no, you remind yourself it's the Earth that's turning, that the workings of the sundial beside the fountain pool incorporate even the sun. Your tea's cooling. What time is sunset anyway? You set down your cup and saucer and doughnut and check your watch. The second hand is just nodding past its zenith.

THE CHESS MUSEUM

*In the square there is the wall where the old men sit and watch the young
go by; he is seated in a row with them. Desires are already memories.*
— ITALO CALVINO, *Invisible Cities*, trans. William Weaver

Amber, ivory, Viking figures, busts of Alekhine, Spassky,
Morphy, oak and walnut boards, boards used by Fischer:

how many years ago did you resolve to bring your questions
to this museum? But first you had the openings to master, knocking

back the Bordeaux through pavement café speed games,
mouthing on about how you'd chased her in all directions

through crowd-ripe boulevards, flea markets, in to the coolness
of the cathedrals that asked you questions you could only

answer with those theology texts you hefted up that foot-worn
staircase with its lattice windows. Stolichnaya chilled to near zero,

each weekend paper with its puzzle waiting on top
of your scholar's garret fridge, sometimes falling open at

the financial section, and so in response you were driven
to hit the clock again and again: your trick was to hopscotch

two steps sideways for each one forwards as you made
your million, uncorking champagne for each rival mastered, your

Wall Street foe emailing you his moves, hinting at new markets
you could only find by travelling to where you sipped

at your Ceylon tea and watched the carved pieces as the last
monsoon droplets splattered from canvas eaves to the leafy floor

somewhere south of Jaffna—what was that creature? Baboon?
Mongoose?—stirring something in you that decided

to build your own straightforward fortress. All the time
you thought this museum a place just about to be discovered,

and so you planned to reach this square a young man,
or shall we say in your prime, but by the time you find yourself

in front of the old illuminated pages with pairs of players
in goldleaf—mediaeval, Arabic, Chinese, Renaissance,

Victorian—you must concede you can only drag your feet
over the tired floor, its marble and granite, one step at a time.

You cannot imagine yourself carrying any pointless questions.
How could you ever have thought them important?

THE COMPUTER MUSEUM

Always, always pelting twenty thousand liquid mice
as Penny parks her Astra. It's been what, nineteen years?
She's first in: unlocks the security grille,
puts on the kettle, sits at her station.

She's designing—no, weaving—her version
of the perfect museum. Her supervisor tells her,
as he tells her every day, to send her plans
to his station by five. And he squeezes her elbow.

Uli's in the virtual room, sporting his headset,
taking her virtual tour of the museum.
His ghost floats past Babbage's adding machine,
diodes of the forties, Texan ghost microchips.

There's the virtual image of the station he's at.
A virtual virtual headset: he's compelled
to make her virtual museum meet reality.
Bound to his virtues. He's no option.

As he's wearing the headset, so must his shade.
The virtual Uli places the virtual virtual headset
on his virtual temples. Presto, at the lobby again.
How many times has he sailed this way today?

At four-forty she erases the last eight hours' work.
She'll apologise to the creep, smile and lock up
a while after he's left. Sirens go wheeling round
in Uli's virtual head, singing what they always sing:

'Always, always pelting twenty thousand liquid mice . . .'

MARY'S CONSEQUENCES

Just how a human heart might warm, it warms you.
Go home. Your family is watching TV.
To the thigh, bone. Wasn't it their parents' flesh,
marrow the gods recycled into the Earth?
I should be your biographer. Make monster

out of you and I'm off this treadmill, these births
and rebirths. Writing how Mary. Met Victor.
On the shores of Lake Geneva. Fold the page.
See how the more I write and fold the paper
the more it makes my voice fade. Dot dot dot dot.

GEARÓID MAC LOCHLAINN

[B. 1967]

SRUTH

I

D'éalaínn go háit rúnda
ar imeall an eastáit tithíochta,
mé i mo bhuachaill,
aonarán ag cuardach tearmainn.

I bpáirc amháin i bhfad ón bhaile
bhíodh abhainn bheag shoilseach
ag stealladh anuas ón chnoc.

Áit gan smál,
í ag drantán ceoil,
mheall sí mé.

Bhíodh plandaí go flúirseach ar a bruacha,
bláthanna gan ainmneacha ag bíogadh,
píobaire fraoigh ag cantaireacht sa raithneach,
suantraí don fhéileacán.

Is san uisce bhíodh brí agus spraoi,
earca inti, glóthach, snáthadáin ag damhsa,
damhán alla ag sníomh gréasáin san fhál,
feithidí ag dordán san aer glan.
Gach rud beo ar a bruacha,
spré don aonarán.

STREAM

I

I used to escape to a secret place
on the edge of the new estate,
a loner seeking shelter.

In a small glen, far from home
was a glistening stream
rushing down from the hills.

Flawless,
humming with music,
it enticed me in.

Plants ran riot along the banks,
nameless flowers waltzing,
grasshoppers crooning in the bracken,
lullaby for butterflies.

In the water, exulting and revelry,
newts, spawn, daddy-long-legs dancing,
spider spinning in the hedge,
insects buzzing in the clear air . . . the ugly bug ball.
All life on the lush banks,
bounty of solitude.

San áit sin chruthaigh mé foraois.
Bhínn ag eitilt
le fáinleoga místiúrtha
mo shamhlaíochta.

II

Lá samhraidh a bhí ann.
D'éalaigh mé
faoi chlúid an chlapsholais.
Bhí port tragóideach an traonaigh le cluinstean,
Mé liom féin, ciotach, faiteach,
chuaigh mé isteach
san uisce.

Faitíos a bhí orm ar dtús
ar eagla go músclóinn spiorad inteacht
ina luí sa dorchadas thíos.
Ach thuirling muinín orm.
Is cuimhin liom é,
mé ag splaiseáil is ag ciceáil mo chos,
buillí boise ar bharr an uisce,
stradúsach, súgach,
croí ar buile,
i bhfad ón bhaile.

III

Níl an sruth ann níos mó.
Tá tithe ina áit.

I forested dreams there.
With the unruly swallows
of imagination
I took to the air.

II

A summer's day.
A gloaming cloaked escape.
To the corncrake's tragic dirge,
alone, awkward, timorous,
I slipped into the water.

At first I was afraid
that I might waken some water spirit
slumbering down there in the murk.
But confidence came,
I remember it now,
splashing and kicking,
slapping the water, straddling, cocksure,
heart gone mad.
Far from home.

III

The stream is gone now.
There are more houses in its place.

Tá na hearca imithe,
an traonach curtha.

Ach táim ag snámh go fóill,
ag sluparnach, ag slaparnach
ar thonn focal,
ag lapadaíl ar chuilithe briathra,
ag ciceáil mo chos
i sruth teangacha.

I mo sheasamh
ar bhruach an Bhéarla atá mé,
ach tá tuile san abhainn,
tuile gan trá,
tá na fáinleoga místiúrtha
athmhúscailte.

Níl faitíos orm níos mó,
leisce ná leithscéal;
rachaidh mé leis an sruth.

The newts have gone for good,
buried with the corncrake.

But I'm still swimming
crashing and plashing
on waves of words,
floundering in a whirlpool of speech,
wading waist deep
in a stream of tongues.

I have been stranded on a levee of English,
but the river is breaking its banks
and the flood seems endless—
unruly swallows
rear up again.

I'm no longer afraid
and my excuses have run dry.
It's time to go with the flow.

[TRANSLATED BY PEARSE HUTCHINSON,
FRANK SEWELL AND THE AUTHOR]

FIRST STEPS

Shiúil muid de choiscéimeanna malltriallacha
suas an lána dorcha chun na scoile gramadaí
mar na saighdiúirí óga gallda ag fágáil slán
le dul chun cogaidh
i ndán Béarla a léigh muid.
Dilly-dallying ár mbealach isteach
mar a thug an múinteoir ranga air.
Bhíodh cumhráin lusanna leanna is giosta
ón ghrúdlann béal dorais ar foluain ar an aer,
ag cigilt na sróine,
is cliunc-clainc maolaithe na gceaigeanna
á lódáil ar na leoraithe Bass.

9.10. Na leabhairíní tanaí bríce-rua os ár gcomhair,
sliabh mistéireach ar an chlúdach,
rud beag cosúil leis an Earagail
ach ní thiocfadh leat bheith cinnte, fiú inniu.
Ag a bhun a thosaigh muid amach
ag siúl go faiteach trí scileach *Is* is *Tá,*
ag dreapadóireacht thar chlocha na haimsire láithrí,
trí chlábar na haimsire caite,
gur shroich muid beanna bána fuara na mbriathra neamhrialta
a thit isteach ar a chéile ina mhaidhm aibítrí.
Is thit muid leo sála in airde, i ndiaidh ár mullaigh,
ag bacadradh linn sa deireadh
go bun an tsléibhe sin arís.

FIRST STEPS

We tortoise-paced our way
up the dark lane to the grammar-school
like the young British soldiers taking leave
in a war poem we read in English class.
'Dilly-dallying' our way in
as the form teacher called it.
The brown sombre smell of hops and yeast
from the brewery next door
hung on the air and jigged the nostrils,
mixing with the muted clunk-clank of kegs
being loaded on the Bass Ireland lorries.

9.10. The slight brick-red books before us,
a mysterious mountain on the cover, something like Errigal
but you couldn't be sure, even today.
We started out at its foot
tippy-toeing shyly through a scree of *Is* and *Tá*,
scaling over bluffs of present tense,
wading inky swamps of the past
until we reached the jutting white peaks of irregular verbs
which imploded in an avalanche of alphabets.
And we toppled with them
head-over-heels and arse-about-face, hobbling dumbly
to the foot of the mountain again.

Feicim go fóill an seanbhráthair
os comhair an chláir dhuibh, riastradh teagaisc air,
cailc ina ghruaig, cailc ina shrón, cailc ina fhabhraí,
cailc faoina ingne,
a shútán dubh anois bán
le stoirm phúdair dhraíochta a thóg sé,
é dár stiúradh mar naíonáin, ag lapadaíl trí mhantra sneachtmhar
an bhriathair *bí.*

NA SCÉALAITHE

Oíche bháistí Aoine ag deireadh Feabhra,
chuinim mionphléascáin an *playstation* nua sa seomra taobh liom
ina bhfuil mo mhac is a chara greamaithe den scáileán teicnidhaite
ina lonnaíonn a chuid teicneo-laochra aeir.
Titeann suan orm.
Luím siar ag aislingiú go n-éirím as mo chorp
ar eiteoga fíneálta snáthadánacha mo chuimhne,
ar foluain mar héileacaptar arm na Breataine
thar shráideanna cúnga m'óige ar an eastát nua.

Clapsholas.
Muid inár mbaiclí, cruinn thart ar lampa sráide briste,
ag cur allais i ndiaidh cluiche *Rap-the-doors* nó *Kick-the-tin*,
ag éisteacht le traonach uaigneach ag screadach sna páirceanna
ar an taobh eile den bhóthar mór,
ag amharc aníos i ndiaidh réalta reatha nó réalta scuaibe
a d'imeodh as radharc chomh gasta
le samhraí m'óige is an traonach glórach féin.

I can still see the old brother
flailing before the black-board in pedagogic frenzy,
chalk in his hair, chalk-filled nostrils,
chalky lashes, chalk beneath the nail,
his black soutane now white
in the twister of magic chalk-dust he summoned
as he guided us like babes,
waddling through
a snowy mantra of the verb *to be*.

[TRANSLATED BY THE AUTHOR]

THE STORYTELLERS

The last Friday in February: it's pouring rain outside,
and I'm getting the flak from the Playstation in the next room
where my son and his mate are glued to the screenful
of techno-heroes locked in technicolored combat.
I must have dozed off, or drifted out of my body
to hover like a British army helicopter
on the viewless wings of poesy
above the planned streets of the new estate.

It's dusk. It's decades ago.
A gang of us have gathered under the smashed street lamp,
breathless after playing Rap-the-doors, or Kick-the-tin,

Anseo faoin lampa briste a shuigh muid—
finscéalaithe an eastáit tithíochta
lenár scéalta leathfhíor, leathchumtha—ár gcuid scéalta cogaidh.
Bhí a fhios againn fiú ansin
go raibh gunnaí curtha faoin chosán,
fite i measc na gcáblaí aibhléise.
Anseo a phléigh muid an t-óglach síoraí
in áiléar tí feirme folamh ar imeall an eastáit,
ag déanamh féasta ar luchóga móra is uibheacha dreoilín,
nó ina luí mar mharbhán, curtha le trí lá
i gcónra urlár adhmaid comharsan ciúine,
gan bhíog as.
Iógaí poblachtach.

Anseo m'anáil íslithe
a chuala mé faoin scuadaí, seacht mbliana déag d'aois,
a chaill cos ag tabhairt cic do channa folamh Coca Cola
inar cuireadh cnaipe bídeach Semtex.
An *para* a chaill a phoill sróine
ag mothú lusa chromchinn i bPáirc na bhFál.
Scéal faoin nóibhíseach
a phléasc é féin ina mhíle píosa thíos ag na dugaí
is a bhí ite suas go hiomlán ag colmáin sráide ocracha
is faoileáin shantacha nár fhág lorg ná rian
do na póilíní is a gcuid bleachtairí.

Pléascann m'óige ionam nuair a chuimhním
ar na poill philéar úra sna brící meirgrua
inar shleamhnaigh muid méara faiteacha,
mar a dhéanfaí ar thaisí naofa
as a dtiocfadh ádh is dea-rudaí dúinn,

ears pricked to the lonesome call of a freight-train
rumbling through the darkened fields beyond the motorway:
a noise which fades as instantly as those stars
we watched fall to earth so many years ago.

Hunkered under the broken lamp,
we were masters of the universe of story,
the legendary half-truths of the war years.
We were clued up to the guns stashed under paving-stones,
clips of bullets sleeved between electric cables.
Here we swore eternal comradeship,
envisaging the empty hay-loft on the frontier of the new estate
where we'd scavenge for rats and wrens' eggs;
or stretch out like corpses
under a neighbour's floorboards for three days,
stiff as boards —
birth-pangs of the revolution.

I held my breath
as I heard the one about the seventeen-year-old Brit
whose leg was blown off when he happened to kick
a pellet-of-Semtex-loaded empty Coke tin.
The para who got an extra hole in his nose
from sniffing coke in the Falls Park.
The rookie volunteer who blew himself to smithereens
down by the docks.
Pickings for the gulls and pigeons:
not a scrap left for Forensics.

is an t-am ar tháinig muid ar raidhfil is gránáid
clúdaithe i saicéadach glas, i bhfolach sna tithe leath-thógtha
ina ndearna muid *base* nuair a bhí sé ag cur
do mhalartú mirlíní is piléir phlaisteacha.
Amanna bhí iontais le feiceáil,
mar an hata círéibe le cealtair
is cumhdach piostail a shábháil na deartháireacha Magee
ó jíp a tiontaíodh bun os cionn
ag cath reatha i lár na hoíche.

Shíl muid go raibh muid saor
mar Khunta Kinte agus Chicken George,
saor mar Kung Fú Cain na feadóige, ag síorshiúl
dhromchla an domhain ghránna, gan eagla.
Saor mar Lin Chung as Liang Shan Po
is lean muid a lorg go mórshúileach,
mar scata moncaithe nite le málaí milseán
os comhair doras draíochta na teilifíse.

Níos moille
fuair muid laochra níos cóngaraí don bhaile,
muid ag malartú
suaitheantas dubh is bán
le haghaidheanna doiléire na stailceoirí ocrais orthu.
Chuir muid de ghlanmheabhair ár dtáblaí iarscoile —

Bobby Sands, May 5, 66 days
Francis Hughes, May 12, 61 days
Raymond McCreesh, May 19, 61 days . . .

Riot after riot,
years of brick walls riddled with fresh bullet-holes
which we prodded with our fingertips
for good luck, like doubting Thomases, wanting to believe.
Swapping marbles and plastic bullets on rainy days at base.
Magnificent trophies,
like the riot helmet and face-shield,
salvaged by the two Magees
from a jeep capsized in an early morning ambush.

We thought we were free,
like Kunta Kinte and Chicken George,
free as cool-fluting Kung Fu Cain
walking the back of the world with no fear,
free as Lin Chung from Liang Shan Po,
dogging his footsteps
like a troop of monkeys munching KP nuts
before the magic portal of the TV.

Before long
we found more down-home heroes.
We swapped black and white badges
Xeroxed with the stark faces
of the men on hunger-strike.
We'd recite them like our times tables:

Bobby Sands, May 5, 66 days
Francis Hughes, May 12, 61 days
Raymond McCreesh, May 19, 61 days . . .

San oíche is mé faoi na braillíní sa dorchadas,
ag éisteacht le fuaimeanna fadálacha diamhra na sráide,
thiontaíodh *tiltswitch* beag ionam
gur shamhlaigh mé íobairtí móra
a dhéanfainn féin do mhuintir Éireann.
Sa nanashoicind idir chodladh is dúiseacht
gheobhainn spléachín den phoblacht órga
mhistéireach le teacht,
sula dtagadh suan orm—

Thomas McElwee, August 8
Mickey Devine, August 20 . . .

Ar maidin bhíodh na sráideanna líonta lán
le *halfers* agus *hickers*, buidéil bhriste, tinte beaga,
púcaí toite liatha, is scéalta, finscéalta,
ráflaí laochra sráide, luaithríona, cumhracht pheitril is rubar dóite
is cnámharlaigh bhusanna Uladh, dóite amach,
ina luí mar chorpáin lofa eilifintí brónacha
a chuaigh ar strae san oíche ar na bóithre dorcha.

Ba leanaí cogaidh muid,
páistí a thuig greann na círéibe,
cumhachtaí draíochta piléar,
castachtaí cruálacha buamaí.
Bhíodh ár mbrionglóidí trom le *binlids* is *barricades*
is taipéis laethanta órga grian-nite samhraidh
fite le *tripwires* na samhlaíochta.

Huddled under my blanket in the dead of night,
I'd tune my ears to the whirrs and clicks of the street,
and feel a little tilt-switch in me turn me on
to dreams of sacrifice for Ireland.
In that twilight zone, for one split chink of time,
I'd glimpse the imminent republic in all its majesty
before sleep wiped it out . . .

Thomas McElwee, August 8
Mickey Devine, August 20 . . .

Come dawn, the streets would be littered
with halfers, broken bottles, tongues of flame
smouldering among the rubble,
muttering of ruins, ashes, rumours, epic escapades,
the whiff of petrol and rubber,
and twisted skeletons of Ulsterbuses
slumped like burned-out mammoths.

We were war urchins,
wise kids, well versed in riotous behaviour.
We knew the amulet powers of the bullet,
the cruel complexion of the bomb.
Our dreams were fraught with barricades and binlids,
the golden tapestry of burning summer days
wrought with the glittering tripwires
of imagination.

[TRANSLATED BY CIARAN CARSON]

CAINTEOIR DÚCHAIS

Táim tuirseach
den *ritual* seo.
Amarc orthu anois,
na daoine bochta,
líne acu réidh
le deoch a cheannach
don rud neamhchoitianta, mistéireach sin.
Rud nach bhfuil cur síos air
sna focail seo—cainteoir dúchais.

Iad cromtha go híseal
os a comhair
mar a bheadh siad i láthair
a slánaitheora.

Agus éist an focalstór atá acu anois,
gach teanga acu
ag coimhlint lena chéile,
ag déanamh seitrince
laistigh dá mbéal.

Agus a leithéid de *name-drop*áil
níor chuala mé riamh.

THE NATIVE SPEAKER

I'm tired
of this ritual.
Just look at them!
Lining up
to buy a drink
for the rare case
I certainly can't describe
in these words —
the native speaker.

See how they bow
down to him
as if they were there
in the presence
of their Messiah . . .

And listen to the word-hoard
they have now,
each one's tongue
competing with the other,
set-dancing away
in their mouths.

And the name-dropping!
You've never heard the like of it.

Agus amharc mo dhuine bocht,
an *genuine article* sin.
Athchruthaíonn siad é
go dtí nach duine é níos mó,
ach rud níos mó ná duine,
rud luachmhar,
seoid i mbéal na muice,
iarsma.

Is anocht beidh amhrán acu,
beár mall acu,
scoth na Gaeilge acu.
Bíodh acu.

Shiúil mé le cailín tráth,
cailín deas dóighiúil.
Ba chainteoir dúchais í
ach bhlais a cuid póg
chomh deas
le póg ar bith eile.

And look at yer man,
the real Mc Coy,
they've transformed him
till he's not even a person anymore
but something more,
something precious,
a jewel in a pig's mouth,
a relic.

And tonight,
they'll have songs,
a late bar,
the best of Irish.
Let them have it.

I once had a girl,
a fine, fit-looking girl.
She was a native speaker
but her kisses tasted
as sweet
as any other.

[TRANSLATED BY FRANK SEWELL]

TEANGA EILE

Mise an teanga
i mála an fhuadaitheora,
liopaí fuaite le snáthaid,
cosa ag ciceáil.

Mise an teanga
sínte ar bhord an bhúistéara
in oifigí rialtais, géaga ceangailte,
corp briste brúite
curtha faoi chlocha
ar chúl claí
roimh bhreacadh an lae.

Mise an teanga
a fhilleann san oíche, ceolta sí, Micí Mí-ádh.
Snámhaim trí na cáblaí aibhléise,
ceolaim os íseal
i bhfiliméad an bholgáin ar do thábla.
Eitlím trí na pasáistí dúdhorcha rúnda
faoin chathair bhriste.

Mise an teanga a sheachnaíonn tú
ar na bóithre dorcha,
i dtábhairní. Croí dubh.
Fanaim ort faoi lampa sráide buí

SECOND TONGUE

I am the tongue
in the kidnapper's sack
lips stitched, feet flailing.
I am the tongue
bound on the butcher's block
in government offices,
a battered, broken corpse
ditched at dawn.
I am the tongue
who comes in the night.
I am a jinx
swimming through flex
and electricity cables.
I sing softly in the element of the bulb
on your table.
I am Johnny Dark, Creole.
I wing through secret pitch-black passageways
beneath the broken city.
I am the tongue
you shun on dark roads, in pubs.
I am hoodoo
waiting for you on the corner
under the yellow street lamp,
stalking you like a jilted John.
I am the tongue
you silenced. I am patois.

ag an choirnéal.
Leanaim do lorg mar leannán diúltaithe.

Mise an teanga a thostaigh tú.
Ortha mé,
i bpóca dubh an fhile choirr
i muinín déirce.

AISTRIÚCHÁIN

(Léamh filíochta, Meán Fómhair 1997)

The act of poetry is a rebel act — HARTNETT

Ní aistriúcháin a chloisfidh sibh anocht, a chairde,
mé aistrithe, athraithe is caolaithe,
le huisce aeraithe an Bhéarla,
a dhéanfadh líomanáid shúilíneach
d'fhíon dearg mo chuid filíochta.
Ní bheidh mé aistrithe anocht.
I mean like, cad chuige a bhfuil mé anseo
ar chor ar bith?

An ea gur seo an faisean is úire?
Léamh dátheangach, *poetry* as Gaeilge.
An ea go bhfuil an saol ag athrú?
Ní féidir a bheith cinnte.

I am mumbo-jumbo, juju,
a mojo of words
in the back pocket
of the weirdo poet
busking for bursaries.

[TRANSLATED BY SÉAMAS MAC ANNAIDH AND THE AUTHOR]

TRANSLATIONS

(Poetry reading, September 1997)

Tonight, my friends, there will be no translations,
nothing trans-lated, altered, diluted
with hub-bubbly English
that turns my ferment of poems
to lemonade.
No, tonight, there will be no translations.
''*Séard atá á rá agam ná*',
what am I doing here anyway?

Is this just the latest fashion, a fad —
the bilingual reading,
poetry '*as Gaeilge*'?
Had the world gone mad?

Sometimes, you get tired talking
to lazy Irish ears. Tired

GEARÓID MAC LOCHLAINN [193]

Amanna, éiríonn tú tuirseach
de chluasa falsa Éireannacha.
Féinsásamh an *monoglot* a deir leat—
'*It sounds lovely. I wish I had the Irish.*
Don't you do translations?'

Iad ag stánadh orm go mórshúileach
mar a stánfadh ar éan corr a chuireann
míchompord de chineál orthu.
Iad sásta go bhfuil sé thart,
sásta go bhfuil an file Béarla ag teacht i mo dhiaidh
le cúpla scéal grinn
a chuirfidh réiteach ar an snag seo san oíche.

Agus seo é anois againn
lena chuid cainte ar '*café culture*' is ar '*Seamus*'.
Seo é le cruthú dóibh go bhfuil siad
leathanaigeanta is cultúrtha,
go dtuigeann siad an pictiúr mór,
go dtuigeann siad filíocht.
Seo anois é.

Agus sin mise ansiúd thall i m'aonar,
i gcoirnéal mo ghruaime,
ag stánadh go héadmhar,
ólta ar fhíon rua mo chuid filíochta,

mo chuid filíochta Gaeilge
nár thuig éinne.

of self-satisfied monoglots who say
—*It sounds lovely. I wish I had the Irish.*
Don't you do translations?

There they are, gawping at me, wide-eyed,
like I'm some kind of odd-ball
just rolled out of lingo-land,
making them all uneasy.
And how glad they are when it's over,
glad the 'English' poet is up next
with a few jokes to smooth over
the slight hitch in the evening.

And here he is
with his talk of 'café culture' and 'Seamus'.
Here he is to prove to them
they are witty, broad-minded and cultured;
that they get the gist of this poetry thing
that tops and tails the evening.
Here he is now.

And there's me in the corner,
alone, dejected,
gawping wide-eyed with jealousy,
drunk on the red wine of my poetry,

my 'Irish' poetry
that no one understood.

[TRANSLATED BY FRANK SEWELL AND THE AUTHOR]

AN MÁINE GAELACH

do m'athair

Ba ghnách linn dul le m'athair,
ar mhaidneacha Sathairn
sula mbíodh na tábhairní oscailte,
chuig siopaí peataí deannacha Shráid Ghréisim.
Uaimheanna dorcha iontais,
an t-aer tiubh le mún is min sáibh
a chuirfeadh na poill sróine ag rince.
Ní bhíodh le cloisteáil istigh
ach fuaim shúilíní ciúine uisce,
glúp ruball éisc
ag tumadh go bun babhla
as radharc ina mionlongbhá rúnda,
seabhrán sciatháin cholmáin shnoite.
Brioscarnach mhistéireach
i measc an fhéir thirim bhuí.
Bhíodh hamstair, geirbilí, luchóga bána
coiníní dubha, pearaicítí buí,
nathracha malltriallacha ina gcodladh céad bliain
mar a bheadh an áit faoi dhraíocht.
Bhíodh an toirtís bhrónach
ag síorgheimhriú,
corntha ina blaosc mhurtallach,
dubh dóite le méara tanaí páistí
ag priocadh ghreille a cáis ghruama.
Ach ba chuma linn

THE IRISH-SPEAKING MYNAH

for my father

Saturday mornings
before pub opening time
my father would take us
to the pet-shops in Gresham Street—
dark Aladdin's caves
reeking of piss and sawdust.
All you could hear in there
was bubbles
or the bloop of a goldfish
diving to the seabed
of its glass world
where it hid behind a pebble,
or a dove gobbling
at its wing feathers
amid a bed of golden crackling straw.
Hamsters, gerbils, white mice,
black bunnies, and canary birds,
sleeping-beauty-serpents;
the melancholy tortoise
in eternal hibernation,
a Rip Van Winkle
fed-up with the grubby mits of kids
poking at it through the wire grille.

faoin chuibhreann Andaithe Falsa Seo
fad is a bhí seisean ann
ag amharc anuas, ó phriocaire te a phéirse
ar an domhan marbh geimhriúil seo,
ag preabadach ó chos go cos
ina chulaith dhúchleiteach chorraithe.
Pótaire de shagart ar a phuilpid,
Áhab ag stiúradh choite an tsiopa
lena chuid bladhmaireachta boirbe.
Mothaím go fóill
a shúil mhire shoiléir
ar casadh ina cheann slíoctha,
mar mhirlín dubh
ag tolladh chúl mo chinn
ag gliúcaíocht orm,
a ghnúis aosta claonta ar leataobh.
Éan corr, mheall sé lena ghlórtha muid,
snagaire de sheanchaí sraoilleach,
a bhéal ar maos le mallachtaí meisceoirí,
eascainí graosta,
focal faire na nÓglach
ó bhallaí Bhóthar na bhFál.
Aisteoir teipthe ag aithris
reitric fholamh na sráide dúinn,
téad ar a chos a cheangail é le
bata scóir a phéirse—
Suibhne ceangailte is cuachta
lena mhearadh focal.

Rinne muid ceap magaidh den gheabaire gaoithe seo
is a fhoclóir cúng sráide,

But no matter about this fool's paradise
so long as *he* was there,
looking quizzically down from his perch
at the comatose world,
shifting from foot to foot
in his dazzling feather boa outfit,
a whiskey-priest in the pulpit,
Ahab steering the pet-shop to perdition
from a crow's next of rant.

I can still see him
jooking at me with his head cocked
to one side,
his mad eye
rolling like a buller in its socket,
boring into the back of my skull.
Quixotic bird, tattered old sea-dog,
he stammered out amazing repartee
and drunken troopers' curses,
all the passwords of the old Falls Road IRA.
Resting actor, stuck to the barstool
of his perch, a veritable Sweeney
tethered by his string of gabble.

We made a laughing stock of this old windbag,
mocked his down-town word-store.
We'd no time for fancy grave orations
so we thrust our sloppy poetry

chuir muid maslaí ar ár n-óráidí tragóideach
is d'fhág muid ár gcuid filíochta slapaí
ar a theanga bhocht bhriste
a bhí líofa tráth
le grág is cá.

PATRÓL

Steallann siad amach as beairic an Springfield,
isteach go Sráid Cavendish, mar a lonnaíonn siad
sna gairdíní os mo chomhair amach,
scata gealbhan i ndufair fhiaileach.
Tuirlingíonn cuid eile ar thairseach eibhir eaglais Naomh Pól,
seabhrán druideanna díothacha,
leathghlas, leath-dhúghorm i mbreacdhuifean spéir an tráthnóna.
Suíonn siad bomaite, comharthaí láimhe ban ag bladhmadh go tapa,
tinte gealáin gallda i mbolg an fháil dhorcha,
cupán na láimhe eile ag muirniú coim néata a raidhfil SA80,
sula mbogann siad go malltriallach suas an tsráid,
líne lachíní ar druil.
Casann ceann acu ar a shála anois is arís
ag breathnú trína threoir theileascópach
le hamas a thógáil ar mharc samhailteach,
ag díriú ar an stócach a thagann as siopa an choirnéil,
nach dtugann aird air.

on his tragic tongue
that was once fluent
with squawk and caw.

[TRANSLATED BY CIARAN CARSON]

PATROL

They pour out of Springfield barracks
into Cavendish St and occupy
positions in front-gardens up ahead —
a flock of sparrows in a tangle of weeds.
A few settle on the granite steps
of St Paul's, whirring like a troop
of hard-up starlings, half-green and blue
in the quick-dim-dusk. They stop
a moment, and suddenly hand-signals
flare up like strange flames in the dark belly
of the hedge, while other hands cup the neat
waist of SA80 assault rifles
before they move on up
the street doing the goosey-gander.
One bad penny spins on his heels every now and then
looking through his telescopic gun-sight
to take aim at some imaginary target,

Chluinim raidió droimphaca,
craobhóga stataigh ag brioscarnach faoi chos,
is cogarnach blasanna Sasanacha ag druidim anall liom.
Fear gorm, déagóir, *beret* ar a cheann,
gealacha dorcha ag crandú i ngealáin a shúl sa leathdhorchadas.
B'fhéidir gur seo a chéad phatról.

—*Awright maite, cold one, innit?* a deir sé liom,

ag claonadh a chinn orm go cairdiúil.
Tá mé reoite bomaitín le hiontas,
mar réiltín scuaibe corraithe as a chúrsa.
Is beag nach labhraím leis
sula scaoilim saigheada searbha nimhe
ó mo shúile stainceacha
is téim thar bráid gan smid asam.

Tá an oíche ag titim,
is roimh i bhfad
beidh súil an tsolais chuardaigh
ag ciorclú ina strób fadálach,
ina dioscó sráide.

Sroichim an coirnéal
mar a ndéanaim comhartha na croise,
is stopaim bomaite taobh amuigh den eaglais
ag machnamh dom féin ar na céimeanna eibhir.
Breathnaím ar an phatról ag dul as radharc
sula ndéanaimse scrúdú coinsiasa gasta,

like the youth coming out of the corner-shop
and paying him no heed whatsoever.

I hear a back-pack radio, twigs
of static crackling underfoot, English
accents, whispering, closing in.
A black soldier, a teenager in a beret,
smouldering dark-moon-eyes.
This could be his first patrol.

—Right mate, cold one innit? he says,

trying to look, or to be friendly.
For a split-second, I'm bowled over,
like a star knocked out of its socket.
I almost answer, before slipping into character.
My eyes aim back a poisoned glance
and I shoot past without a word.

Dark is falling, and soon
a searchlight will begin its dervish dance,
a slowed-strobe discoing the narrow streets.

I reach the corner and cross myself,
halting a moment on the granite steps
of the chapel.
Looking back at the patrol disappearing
from view, I rifle my conscience, briefly.

tá mé buartha
go sílfidh an scuadaí gorm óg,
gealacha dorcha ag crandú
ina shúile
gur *racist* mé.

OÍCHE SHATHAIRN SA CHATHAIR

Tá an beár plódaithe,
an fhoireann faoi bhrú.
Ní fhaca Ritchie, fear an tí, gnó mar seo le bliain anuas:
you'd think the ceasefire was on again, a deir sé.
Tiontaíonn sé, ag gáire, i dtreo bheirt bhan bhorba
ar tí gearán faoin mhoill ar dheoch.
Yes ladies? Bladhmann an bladar díreach in am.

I gcoirnéal toiteach, ag cúl an tí,
pléascadh scigireachta,
na buachaillí beorach ag déanamh mionléirmheasa
ar ghreann graosta,
báite i gcumhracht rúnda slaite *marijuana*
a athríonn ó láimh go láimh go ciúin
faoin tábla,
mar phláta ofrála.

What if the young black squaddy
with smouldering dark-moon-eyes
thinks I'm some kind of racist?

[TRANSLATED BY FRANK SEWELL AND THE AUTHOR]

SATURDAY NIGHT ON THE TOWN

The bar is packed,
the staff run off their feet.
Ritchie the publican hasn't done
business like this all year:
'You'd think the ceasefire was on again,' he says.
He turns smiling to a couple of tough biddies
poised to give out about the delay on drink.
'Yes, ladies?' Soft soap in the nick of time.

In a smoky corner at the back
scoffing erupts,
beer-boys picking holes in dirty jokes,
wreathed in incognito-fragrances of hasheesh joints
passed from hand to hand,
quietly, under the table,
like a collection-plate.

Tá scata beag cruinnithe thart ar an cheol i lár an tí,
cinn ag luascadh ar shreanga dofheicthe.
That's a session! a deir cailín ólta taobh liom.
A *wake for King Rat,* a deir a cara.
Tá na ceoltóirí tógtha le teocht is teasaíocht
an scata fhiabhrasaigh.
Teannann siad ar ríl fhiáin. Conairt bhuile.
Uaill chaointe ó na píoba. Cuimhne eitilte.
Déanann méara damhsa mire damháin alla chiaptha
ar mhuineál caol maindilín.

Tá na doirse druidte. An teach lán.
Ar feadh tamaill dhraíochta éalaímid
ó bhrú ceannlínte nuachta,
ó mhearbhall na seachtaine.
Táimid linn féin. Eaxodus ceolmhar
i gcumann bhé an drabhláis.
Imirce oíche.

Lasmuigh, áit inteacht sna scáthanna fuara,
slingeadóir gunna óg eile ag fanacht
le croí diúltach mífhoighneach.

Druideann na spéartha go gasta,
ag dlúthú mar sceachaill dhorcha
os cionn na cathrach.

There's a cluster of punters round the session,
heads bobbing on unseen strings.
The crowd's fever infects the music.
They lurch into a wild reel,
a pack of hounds picking up the scent.
The pipes wail. Winged memories.
On the snug oak neck of the mandolin
fingers do a stressed-out spider's crazy quickstep.

The doors are closed. The house full.
For a magic while we escape
the pressure-cooker of headlines,
the vertigo radio reports.
We are alone. A musical exodus.
A moonlight flit with Bacchus
at the wheel.

Outside, somewhere in the cold shadows,
waits another young gunslinger,
his heart hardened, impatient.

The skies close down quick,
tightening over the city
like a dark tumour.

[TRANSLATED BY PEARSE HUTCHINSON
AND THE AUTHOR]

AG FIRÉADÁIL

D'éalaíodh sé uaim,
ag doirteadh trí mo mhéara spréite
mar rópa uisce reatha beo beathach.
Watch 'im. He has the smell, a deireadh m'athair liom.
D'fhéachainn a mhearadh fola místiúrtha,
na súile nimhneacha bándearga ag lonrú;
diabhal bídeach craosach
ar thóir anamacha.

D'éalaíodh sé uaim,
an poll síos,
rian trom muisc
óna chuid fionnaidh dheannachúil, neamhnite,
ag smálú mo bhoise foilmhe,
é ag srónáil go tostach
go croí te an choinicéir,
deoraí ag filleadh ar a fhód,
ag lúbarnaíl trí shíbíní dorcha
a dhúchais dhiamhair féin,
a dhomhain faoi thalamh,
ar lorg na fola a shásódh a mhian,

file fiáin, ocrach,
ag fiach greim focal
i ndoimhneacht
chanúint na gnáthóige.

FERRETING

He'd slip away from me,
Run through my open fingers
Like a rope of live water.
'Watch him. He has the smell,' my father would say.
And I could see the wild blood-rush in him,
His pink pearl eyes gleaming;
A greedy wee demon
Hungry for souls.

He'd slip away from me
Down the hole,
The stink of his dusty, unwashed fur
Musking my empty palm
As he nosed his way
To the warm heart of the warren
Like an exile coming home,
Twisting and turning
Through the dark snugs
Of his own mysterious kingdom,
His underground world,
Seeking out blood
to wash his mind.

A restless poet, clawing and hungering,
Trying to catch hold of a word or a phrase
Deep in the dialect of lair.

[TRANSLATED BY FRANK SEWELL AND THE AUTHOR]

FRANK SEWELL

[B. 1968]

NOT KNOWING WHERE YOU STAND

is where you stand;
always wanting to put your foot down
on dry land and not finding it
or, when you do, not standing it,
sailing on until you change
your mind, turn back and find it gone.

Is it under a pebble or stone
scooped up and dropped into the ocean,
your one-and-only chance
which when recognised as such
hightails it? Where do you stand
when you're too far-gone to judge
the swell of the sea, the lie of the land?

TRIPTYCH

I

You took yourself off. Another surprise
that should not have surprised us.
You always liked to do your own thing
if you could. And you could in some things.

Just like that, your heart stopped.
The dog you let sleep on your bed
must have howled with animal hurt,
the way I did when I heard.

Your brother called me son, he was so sorry
for my trouble. The day you died,
a grave in me opened and, already buried,
you came back to me. Another surprise.

II

Nothing I got from you that wasn't broken.
Just now, a crack and clatter across the work-top
as something goes flying.
I have to search the floor to see what.
And there it lies:
a big blue plastic spoon,
part of a set that no longer sits
on its mooring, the frail stand
you picked up, no doubt, for a bargain.
Now I pick up the stray from the floor,
dunk it in the basin—a quick lick.
What shall I do with it?
I've tried before to glue the arm
that holds it to the rest of the set
but the join keeps breaking under the weight.
Better to let them all lie flat in a drawer
out of sight like you in your grave.
Nothing I got from you that wasn't broken.

Or that I haven't kept—
the camera I brought all the way to Gdansk,
the personal organiser with the Union Jack.
Nothing I got from you that wasn't broken.
Like the gift of life itself,
your health, our home and, in the end, your heart.
Nothing I got from you that wasn't broken.
But it wasn't your fault the glue didn't last
or the whole equal the sum of the parts.
It doesn't always.

III

Now I remember our last phone-call,
how you told me you loved me,
and I wondered was it the whiskey,
decided it was, reaching for the word
as you would the reality.

As easy for me to put it down
to that as for you to down
drink, or me the phone and cut
the conversation with the thought,
I can't talk to you like that.

It was almost the last chance we got,
the first in ages to talk one
to one. I promised I would call
you back, meaning *get off the phone*
and *don't call me again at work.*

HANDS

One hand so loved sand,
he wrapped himself around
as many of the golden grains
as he thought he could contain.

On guard against loss,
his fingers grew solid as walls,
his palm hard as prison floors,
his thumb shut tight as the door.

Even then, sand breezed
through the cracks, released
itself to the open air, drifted
to the beach. The hand stiffened.

Feeling his hoard, once soft,
unfill his grasp and grow rough,
he tightened his hold and clasped
together joints, folds, gaps

so hard he sensed every loss.
His efforts crushed and forced
the last of his treasure
away. Easing the pressure,

his wrist sagged with relief,
fingers, half-dead or asleep,

stretched out, his thumb woke.
Fingernails to palm, he shook.

Sand fell away from him
inevitably as time,
and he was left as if
losing was his life.

Another hand so loved sand,
he held it loosely for a moment,
then let it go, free.
The hand was soon empty

and himself free to hold
more sand; not the old
grains scattered to the winds
but infinitely varied combinations

again and again until
he embraced the cold thrill
of empty space, the freedom
and contrast it gave him.

YOUR PELT PYJAMAS

are small
but beautiful
the breast pockets

full of change
and the trousers
always manage
to wind up
tuckcd into
my own
the two
woven
into one
at the waist
feet or knee
not that this
is any kind
of complaint
believe me
whatever it is
is going on
between your
pelt pyjamas
and my own
I don't want
undone

CRUMLIN

Crumlin—something 'bend' or 'stoop'?
For me, a place where the train pulls up
and, unnoticed, the ghost of you slips

into my carriage, through my lips
and under my skin where you belong
but will not stay. By Glenavy, you're gone.

Then Belfast, the 'Farset-Mouth' closed
to us, all those deadly momentos,
old haunts where it hurts to go
or look back at an empty window.
A day at most, and I return
to Coleraine, hideaway, 'corner of fern',

and again have to pass through Crumlin.
How can I get round you, woman?
Wipe Crumlin off the map?
Hijack the train and never stop?
Blow the whistle, shoot on past
the people and prams? Not so fast.

With the seven powers invested in me
by Crom's Three Hags of the Long Teeth,
I'll crumple Crumlin to a speck
thrice bound in a haversack
with lace from a girl's DM boot,
the gold wristwatch of King Canute,

and a bobble you bunched her hair with once.
Now it's worse than it ever was.
The train misses out Glenavy to Antrim,
and I feel there's something wanting,
something lost that can't be regained,
spirited away like the *gh* in *Cromghlinn*.

FOR SEÁN Ó RÍORDÁIN

1

Remember the days
you could hang a poem
on the sun's rays?
You didn't give a damn,
it was that natural.
Verse flew through you
like a dose of salts
or a bad flu,
making you cough
shadows from your lungs.
More reason than enough
to spit, you sung.

2

Dark, there from day one,
lets there be light.
Inherence, is that it?
The way there's no ocean
except where stones cut
waves like a vandal's knife,
or the bulb over this hut
flicks on/off all night?

Here's a black spot, Sean.
Are you following me?
I could have sworn . . .
What about the pub for company?
No, you're right about that.
Not worth a shilling,
the half-words and -thoughts
passed in lieu of conversation
there. Who am I telling?

I like this outdoor condensation,
the wind slugging my coat
and hat, the night pitch-black,
and you following me about.
Cohen says everything's cracked,
that's 'how the light gets in'.

Look! That bulb flashing
bright-not-bright again,
the tipsy rain dancing
on The Anchor, the boats,
the naff bedighted lamp-posts,
and shops watching from the Prom,
the on/off/on/off/on
of a beaming, being, breathing
absence, presence of light
that keeps coming or leaving—
it's too hard to decide
with no tense in English

for the *bíonn/ní bhíonn*
there still be's in Irish
from Gaoth Dobhair to Dún Chaoin.

3

Sean, Galltacht and Gaeltacht
speak a forked tongue.
It's for priests, not poets,
to chant a plain song.

Listen, can I be honest?
I learnt from Ó Direáin
to learn from Yeats;
and still I am learning

from fathers and artificers
who have flickered since Joyce
took language, lit the face of her,
and showed us up in words.

PAUL GRATTAN

[B. 1971]

MIDDLE

FROM *The Municipal Family Revisited*

In Gran's house, a plastic swan from Saltcoats kept
watch inside the alcove. Wings made bouquets of daffodils
phlegm-quilled in their yellowed dustcoat plume.

Well-fired morning rolls would hatch from white
paper bags like dinosaur eggs, in the Ladybird books
she read me. Two halves of breakfast, *brake* and

fast, forever severed by the standard Habbie of her
tongue. *Elizabeth the first of Scotland and her retinue
dropped by the Barrhead Road around the time yon toe-rag*

Teddy Taylor was in Castlemilk. With the clarity of one
who has abdicated motor functions, she minds the Corpy
planting silver birch, skin-deep in tar-macadam.

PIPE DREAM

Daft bastard never realised you could hear fuck all
for the noise of the lathe, his luck turning at eighteen hundred revs,
a fool on a rough feed ripping chunks out of a democratically

elected Communist government—*Get aff the soap the box ya clown,*
these X's'll burn your fuckin eyes out—a worthless gesture,
grating against the bight of the chuck, the perspex faceguard
smothering all congress. We stopped the feed, pulled back
the cross slide freeing the fool and switched off the machine.

Then I felt we had betrayed him, in the rubble of the Moneda,
a sell-out crowd for the end of season game—*At least play*
tae the whistle, brother, if ye canny write tae the bone.
If you ask them in La Legua, Victor Jara should go home.

Swarfega'd palms sud memories of a wee, decent man
whose Party we compared with the Sunday Post—*shite paper*—
three days later his neck struck our hard logic and snapped,
the pipe still in his hand. His soul arced through the air,
showering us both with hot ash.

DESCARTES AT IBROX

for Martin Mooney

Check him, some waster waxing lyrical in a bar,
chinned by a bear in Rangers colours for failing
to hum ardently the air to Derry's Walls; this *per se*
would not seem unusual. Except it didn't happen

Qua rammy. Injuries were sustained as a result
of paper cuts to the left nostril, inflicted when said Hun
proclaimed Hume's rebuttal of the French Man to be
epistemologically speaking, *fucking out of order.*

Coming to, reverse angle replays show two tattooed
fists insist on their existence, above and beyond the temple
of the Copeland Road Stand. Man marked, out the game
the upward trajectory of his meditations proved fatal.

IN SITU

from A TYPICAL CELL

A nurse has taken pity and the time to find me
coffee, while they prep you for the table with a
viscous yellow rub. Surgeon and Anaesthetist
differ on the risk you pose expensive, fraught
procedures and the limits to your blood. At half-

past three a plastic screen is circled round your
morphined lids. A junior Doctor waves her gold
tipped nib across some document and inks out
a release. Morphine signs on your behalf then
dandles down two tubers, protruding from your wrist

and middle finger. Swabs of artificial light
decline an article I read on *Cancer and You, the facts*.
Freesias someone left you wither at the window
like they want to get out and I can't kiss you
for catheters, stinking, waiting to be fixed.

A LITTLE NIGHT MUSIC

... still they are only us younger. —ROBERT LOWELL

I. A MARXIST SENDS A POSTCARD HOME

Last night they took our drainpipe for the bonfire
and it's only May—which just goes to show uncle Tam
knew hee-haw about seasonal politics. So now rain
rivets the pavement instead of trickle-down. Rats rave
in the attack to the helicopter's three a.m. arias
and the party in my head won't stop. *Who will raise
a glass to our broken faces and see this place?*

When we were weans I chased her campaign Ford
Cortina round the cottage flats and semi's of Croftfoot.
Election night in Donegal Pass brings back the way
you lashed an aspirant 'h' between the 'c' and 'u' of 'cunt'
whenever talking Tory. We both have drunk and downward
dragged the deeply bearable. Nudged now towards
new labours, we'd better work our better halves to death.

II. NORTH QUEEN STREET, *MON AMOUR*

All night she brandishes the bread-knife
and brand new hammer. The handle of which
has just been chewed by the stray she strokes
in sympathy. The big black lab cross that eats
and shits its way through Giros, like it was going
back to work. Crouching on the arm of the carved
up Chesterfield copy, red and white barber's
curtains shut as much as rails askew allow,
she girns aloud—*if you took a hammer*
to those weans who shimmy and clamber
over smouldering bread boxes on the York Road
mouthing, 'who you slabberin to now', how
long would it take the hacket wifie in 236
who breeds the wee bastards to haul herself
out of the North Star and into her slacks;
to pucker up in front of the cameras, tearfully
confide that our Lyndsey was the life and soul
of the party; that the child benefit will be sorely
missed by all who knew her; that she was only
fifty Focus Points off a B & H bath towel
when the dear Lord took her for one of his own.

III. THE END OF NAPOLEON'S NOSE

Tonight we are folding ours sins into newspaper,
drowning our chips in malt vinegar from ginger bottles
outside the Golden Sea. The naturally saturated high
of fish suppers in transit, nasal napalm for the blind.

At the back of the mind, dole-queues swell like poppers,
trips liquefy shelf lives in showers of six o'clock shoppers.
We lick fingers, salty from other fuckers' wounds, testing
The products' unfamiliar skin. Impeccably dressed

for the price of a can we might kill the horsey-set pigs —
a scene out of Dostoevsky — black tongued Bulgarian wine
drinkers' sons in combat boots with flak-jacket faces
dragging a donkey down the waterworks to see if it floats.

Belfast fills with ghosts. Greyhounds' sport coats to keep
the dogma out. We toss and dream of ice-cream, the virtues
of dirty women, until solvent at last, it's time to pick
one half of eglantine, at the end of Napoleon's nose.

NO SECOND FRY, COOKSTOWN, FEBRUARY 24TH 2000

She too eschews a surface patience, preparing to chew
in dentured indigence her buttered stick of soldiers,
having first arranged two sausage on a side-plate. Isabel's
café and clothes shop combined. Behind the hot glass
lurk rashers, great lobes of grease curled inwards

in coronary prayer. Eggs stare igneous and jaundiced
as beans bake on their own ring, pushed beyond use,

a callus against appetite. Downstairs my wife is fishing
for tights in bargain buckets. I barter my boiled tomato,
a last isosceles of soda bread surpassing expectations.

Buried under a stew of pramless mothers, her blue rinsed
coral plateau takes the biscuit. You might think images
of ageing would be less frivolous — lines of mean winter
tempered with equal amounts of sunshine — instead, ah
Isabel, caustic in rancid knickers, waiting for Ostend to fall.

THE SEVEN RABBIE BURNS'S
BAD FAITH COME BACK TOUR

His ill-fitting, glossy black cloth, ungainly presence and sharp, dark
vulpine features had in them the vulgarity of a Glasgow artisan in his
Sabbath suit. [FROM *Uncle Silas*, BY SHERIDAN LE FANU]

We never really knew exactly who was being held hostage
or why, synchronised, we sang in the accent of the captor

opening the heart of Andreas Baader. As if we birled to kiss
the cross the day they took out brother Ross, the *Guinness Book*

of Records gawping openly that next night on the News at Ten.
Full of Eastern Promise, we played support to The Thanes of Lauder

during the rain of the Year of Culture. The greatest hit
we never had, a cover off Steak & Kidney's *Govan Cross* L.P.,

Seven Syllables' On the Death of Deng Xiao Ping.
We like to call it, Sweet And Sour Balls Gone Tae Seed.

MAXIM

in memory of Hywel Thomas, philosopher

And if we should be refused trousers
or find ourselves foutering under stars,
exiled by grocers' daughters, in Cuban
heels, a high-heel without curves, better
to have been tarred and feathered in the great
balloon fire of 1785 than suffer this closure,
half out of our patent leathered minds.

You kill me, roaring, tautologies of fuchsia
and blackthorn have emptied our bellies,
binding our hyperborean arse cracks to the wind.
My manqué, my melancholic manqué, go on
in your virtue, save the wails, the wind eggs
and a thousand dule-tree flowers, for the want
of a kind word, John Knox looking on.

SINÉAD MORRISSEY

[B. 1971]

HAZEL GOODWIN MORRISSEY BROWN

I salvaged one photograph from the general clear-out, plucked
(Somehow still dripping) from the river of my childhood.
You in your GDR-Worker phase, salient, rehabilitated:
Reagan, you can't have your Banana Republic and eat it!
Your protest banner and your scraped back hair withstood the flood.
I've hung your smile beside your latest business card: *Nuskin Products*.

Contact address: Titirangi, New Zealand. Out there a psychic
Explained how, in a previous life, I'd been *your* mother,
Guillotined during the French Revolution. You were my albino son.
You saw fire in the windows. This time round we returned to the garrison —
Swanned round Paris in the summer playing guess-your-lover.
I wonder how many of our holidays have closed down cycles.

Anyway, I believe it. Because when you drove to the airport
And didn't come back, it was déjà vu. And I had to fight,
As all mothers do, to let you go. Our lived-in space
Became a house of cards, and there was nothing left to do but race
For solid ground. You settled your feathers after the flight
In a fairytale rainforest. Discovered the freedom of the last resort.

LEAVING FLENSBURG

This city settled on you in layers of days
That brought a grounding with them, that sense of knowing
Where your feet belonged. Memory built the way
In which you recognised the place, decided how much your going
Would cost: a few confused days in the next stop-over, or dreamscape for
    a year.

This one was a hard one to guess, because although
Your feet knew all the town's directions,
And tapped their way through the map they'd got to know,
They never saw their own reflection
In the Baltic harbour: the thousand jellyfish that swarm in in September

Made the glass shiver and the sky disappear.
All the same, you had the Glucksburg Autumn, days when the gold
Set loose in the sky seemed almost like a crime. You feared
The winter, but it came, and the darkness and cold
Brought with them skies of stars, high over Schleswig-Holstein, singing
    in space.

Above all, the shipyard rocketed the price—
Freezing and full of sad men welding steel. It was almost dark
As the finished freighter slid out to the sea, and the thin ice
Cracked in the shapes of flowers, all the way to Denmark.
It was then you knew there'd be dreams for years.

RESTORATION

1. *Achill, 1985*

Once I saw a washed up dolphin
That stank the length of Achill Sound,
Lying on the edge of Ireland.
The Easter wind ripping it clear
Of all its history,
And the one gull watching it,
Abandoned by the tide.
I remember how its body,
Opened in the sun,
Caught me,
And I remember how the sea
Looked wide and emptied of love.

2. *Juist, 1991*

The North Sea booms tonight
And there are no lights the length
Of the fifteen mile beach,
And no stars

The sea is revealing itself
By its own light light revealing
Essences of light:
Meeresleuchten, lights of the sea

One touch and the water explodes
In phosphorescence
No one knows if it lives
It is as though God said

Let there be light in this world
Of nothing let it come from
Nothing let it speak nothing
Let it go everywhere

IN BELFAST

I

Here the seagulls stay in off the Lough all day.
Victoria Regina steering the ship of the City Hall
in this the first and last of her intense provinces,
a ballast of copper and gravitas.

The inhaling shop-fronts exhale the length
and breadth of Royal Avenue, pause,
inhale again. The city is making money
on a weather-mangled Tuesday.

While the house for the Transport Workers' Union
fights the weight of the sky and manages
to stay up, under the Albert Bridge the river
is simmering at low tide and sheeted with silt.

I have returned after ten years to a corner
and tell myself it is as real to sleep here
as the twenty other corners I have slept in.
More real, even, with this history's dent and fracture

splitting the atmosphere. And what I have been given
is a delicate unravelling of wishes
that leaves the future unspoken and the past
unencountered and unaccounted for.

This city weaves itself so intimately
it is hard to see, despite the tenacity of the river
and the iron sky; and in its downpour and its vapour I am
as much at home here as I will ever be.

THE INHERITING MEEK

Your letter comes with the news that the lake blooms
earlier each year. As yet September is free of it,
but then as though *October* were carcinogenic,
and days could split degrees between them evenly,
the oncogene of the lake turns manic
as soon as the month names change. America storms, the world warms
and a soft algal stretch is beginning its reach

from the shadow of your cabin to the stone-stacked beach.
It shows the time-consuming ambition of the inheriting meek.

You say you lost millennial Christmas in a week
spent injecting the lake with oxygen,
and write a list of the wars you've fought with the dam
so far and lost, that were not as bad as this—
giardia, sabotage, evaporation,
the year of no rain when the lake drained to wrecks,
water skis, exhausted eels, a hub cap off your station wagon,
and Aucklanders brought their children
to stare at the reason for rationing.

This could mean a green undrinkable eye in the face
of the forest, the irreversible failure of the water supply,
whilst the language of the luminous algae
is murmurous, like intestines, and quaintly victorious.
Stars miss themselves in the eye, but keep their trajectory.
How neat, you say, and mean it, abhorring stasis,
all change is good. We are piling into a future
we will not escape from easily, if ever,
for we have eaten time. The algae gather.

FEBRUARY

for Kerry Hardie

There is no kindness in me here. I ache to be kind, but the weather
makes me worse. I burrow and sneer. I stay small, low, cheap, squander

all signs of the thaw by screwing my eyes. It's easier in the dark.
Defeat is the colour of morning, the grey that engenders the
 honeymoon flats

and the chessboard of rice fields between this block and that.
Each field is marked

for the administering of cement, this month or the next.
I am living in boom, before the door frames are in or the driveways
 drawn.

The new exit from the station to the south
makes Nagoya spread, calls it out further than one city's insatiable
 mouth

could dream. Factories chew through a mountain beyond my window
and each time I look at it it's less. In the world before the war

this place was famous, a stopping house for the tired and sore.
There was one road only in Japan, and all who walked it walked through

this town. There are photographs of women in an amber light
stopped dead in their surprise at being captured as the image of a time.

Behind them all, the mountain rises white.
They say it stayed so all winter long, a shut door to the north.

The snow scatters now without it. When all the fields are town,
the mountain stones, it will be spring, and I'll be called on

to be generous. There will be days when fruit trees, like veterans
left standing here and there in pools of shade, will forget about use
    and bloom.

GENETICS

My father's in my fingers, but my mother's in my palms.
I lift them up and look at them with pleasure —
I know my parents made me by my hands.

They may have been repelled to separate lands,
to separate hemispheres, may sleep with other lovers,
but in me they touch where fingers link to palms.

With nothing left of their togetherness but friends
who quarry for their image by a river,
at least I know their marriage by my hands.

I shape a chapel where a steeple stands.
And when I turn it over,
my father's by my fingers, my mother's by my palms

demure before a priest reciting psalms.
My body is their marriage register.
I re-enact their wedding with my hands.

So take me with you, take up the skin's demands
for mirroring in bodies of the future.
I'll bequeath my fingers, if you bequeath your palms.
We know our parents make us by our hands.

LULLABY

When I can't sleep, you speak to me of trees.
Of the bald-eyed Eucalyptus
that flared in your back yard
like an astounded relative —
pointing to the honey bees in their rickety hives
your brother had abandoned.

Sometimes the tree was avuncular.
Arch with its secrets.
How it boasted, on days
your mother
hung sugarwater,
the delicate surgery of humming birds.

CONTRAIL

Nightly now, insomnia lays its thumb
upon my forehead—an any how, Ash Wednesday cross.
Which, instead of insisting *Thou Shalt Pass*

to the Angel of Anxiety, hovering over the stairway,
beckons it in, at 3am, to unsettle me gently
with its insidious wings

Sometimes my mother and father.
Sometimes neither.
Sometimes childlessness, stretching out into the ether

like a plane

THE GOBI FROM AIR

1

Auden's face in age
looked like this place.

The same wind-chiselled flair.
The same doubt as to where

decorousness
really ought to begin and end.

Ten thousand barrels of sand
overturned

on the streets of Beijing in a year.
Some days they fear

that the earth
is raining.

2

His addiction to war
delivered him here—

a three-month-old letter
wherever he went.

His trains all avoided the front.
The Japanese shielded their eyes

from the sun, and kept on killing.
He toured warehouses, brothels, remembering,

out of everything,
damp fungus frothing

on the fingertips
of the mill girls in Shanghai.

ADVICE

You think it ugly: drawing lines with a knife
Down the backs of those writers we exist to dislike. But it's life.

One is disadvantaged by illustrious company
Left somehow undivided. Divide it with animosity.

Don't be proud—
Viciousness in poetry isn't frowned on, it's *allowed*.

Big fish in a big sea shrink proportionately.
Stake out your territory

With stone walls, steamrollers, venomous spit
From the throat of a luminous nightflower. Gerrymander it.

ZERO

for Joseph

Whatever else it was he stole from the East—
indigo, gold, a brace of abused and temporary women,
frankincense, the inevitable spice or two,
or the fruit that shed itself with such feral sweetness

on the tongue it begged re-naming —
Alexander also stowed nothing —
that double nick in the Babylonian plaque which,
of everything, was the easiest to store
(the women were a nightmare)
precisely because it lived nowhere
and therefore everywhere: in two spare horseshoes
angled together, in the kiss of a thumb and forefinger,
in the sigh at the bottom of a poured-out water jar,
in the memory of some noon-white city square
wherever luck ran out, or faith, or anger —
                                                but
when Alexander delivered zero to the Greeks
they turned and saw (or thought they saw)
a wellhead blacken in front of them —
an incredulous, bricked-in 'O' —
unravelling into inkiness like a sleeve, the kind
you might toss a stone into and never hear the splash,
though you stand and wait, your ear awash in silence,
for an hour — and over it the bric-a-brac of kitchens appeared
suspended in the sunshine — knives, lemons, sieves, pots, bowls —
a funnel of dailyness, which the wellhead then swallowed
like a child, and, sensing where it could lead,
this number/no-number that would eat the world,
the Greeks turned back to Alexander in the advancing shade
and smiled: for there were still angles, there were still
three old angels skipping over heaven carrying harps and signs.

ALAN GILLIS

[B. 1973]

THE ULSTER WAY

This is not about burns or hedges.
There will be no gorse. You will not
notice the ceaseless photosynthesis
or the dead tree's thousand fingers,
the trunk's inhumanity writhing with texture,
as you will not be passing into farmland.
Nor will you be set upon by cattle,

ingleberried, haunching, and haunting
with their eyes, their shocking opals,
graving you, hoovering and scooping you,
full of a whatness that sieves you through
the abattoir hillscape, the runnel's slabber
through darkgrass, sweating for the night
that will purple to a love-bitten bruise.

All this is in your head. If you walk
don't walk away, in silence, under the stars'
ice-fires of violence, to the water's darkened strand.
For this is not about horizons, or their curving
limitations. This is not about the rhythm
of a songline. There are other paths to follow.
Everything is about you. Now listen.

TRAFFIC FLOW

Letters from Vow and Moneydig are sent to Baltic Avenue,
while from Friendly Row parcels are sent to Drumnakilly
and to Tempo. From Whitehead, past Black Head, and up
to Portmuck, Byron steers his bright red van, dreaming of
Sara in Economy Place, whose handheld has just gone dead.
Down on Cypress Avenue, Katie from Downhill texts Conrad,
lingering in Joy's Entry, listening to *Here Comes the Night*.
She keys 'Sorry but I had 2' while the busker, Sharon, thinks
of phoning home to Gortnagallon. On Dandy Street somebody's
Da says to somebody's Ma: 'Come on to fuck.' It's good to talk.
Moneyglass fills with disillusion. Everybody scampering under
the same weather, crossing lines, never coming together.

LAST FRIDAY NIGHT

So there wi were like, on the fuckin dance
floor an the skank was fuckin stormin like,
shite-posh, but we'd fuckin chance
it, great big fuckin ditties bouncin, shite,
an thighs, skirts wi fuckin arses man, tight,
that ye'd eat yer fuckin heart out fer. I
was fuckin weltered an Victor was ripe
aff his head cos we'd been round wi Johnny
like, downin the duty-free fuckin gargle, aye.

Anyway, wee Markie must've taken
a few a tha aul disco biscuits like,
loved up da fuck, going like a mad yin
when some dicklicker came over like, for a fight.
Slabberin! So the fuckin lads go 'right!'
an a huge fuckin mill-up started but
I fucked aff when this tit's head cracked aff a light.
Fuck sake like, my knuckles are still cut.
Shame ye wernie there, ya nut.

DELIVERANCE

Even the trees are on something.
Somebody, somewhere, is almost
making love. Clouds target the hillside,
bringing water, looking for all the world
like spaceships trying to beam themselves down.
Leaves are trapped by the bars of their branches
and aeroplanes guard the blue, as you try
to break through the green prison of your eyes.
Everyone is going to get off.

■

Unfortunately there are no positions left,
he said. For the record, what can you do?
Somebody, somewhere, is making a killing.

Cigars leer across barstools, asking for a light
now the Sky has been taken from your house.
Then a briefcase tries to sell you up the river.
You shoot the breeze. He talks of a message:
there'd be something in it, all you need do is deliver.

∎

The addicted trees are hooked
on the air. Somebody, somewhere,
is inventing a cure.
Everyone inside is bustling to break out
and the sun has served its time.
Wet dreamers of wide profit margins
drive below the golfball moon,
their speakers selling them life
style options, while you are lying
low. Thieves and lovers gamble in your eyes.

∎

There is a rustling without the windows,
a tinkling in your ear. And somebody,
somewhere, is saved by a machine.
In your dreams you speak to free
heartbeats, dipsticks, ice-floes, smart bombs,
moon men, wolfhounds, death pints,
blue chips, close weather, stem cells, burning discs
and worldwide searches. You speak of bonds.

∎

You wake behind the sun and make
your delivery. There is nothing
in it. The ground beneath your feet
rotates. The planes are on patrol.
Something flies into the pane and dies.
A breeze blows in and everybody profits.
Somebody, somewhere, will understand.
Rub the blue eyes of your windows.
Love is making trees.
You are green under turquoise skies.

UNDER THE WEATHER

The rain? Don't talk to me about the rain.
A slash of sequins, turning to a drilled
downpour of teeth, gnawing the windowpane,
flushing the roof, gaping the spectrum again.
And we walk the waterbulbs, watching rilled
gutterstreams upsplurge, jetsprouting the drain,
our lagoon-heads pealing into thunder.
Sometime soon, we must talk about the thunder.

PROGRESS

They say that for years Belfast was backwards
and it's great now to see some progress.
So I guess we can look forward to taking boxes
from the earth. I guess that ambulances
will leave the dying back amidst the rubble
to be explosively healed. Given time,
one hundred thousand particles of glass
will create impossible patterns in the air
before coalescing into the clarity
of a window. Through which, a reassembled head
will look out and admire the shy young man
taking his bomb from the building and driving home.

KILLYNETHER

Each time I ignore the stranger in the mirror
on the big wardrobe door, and open wide
its lacquered hatches, lured by the whiff
of dark hanging coats, their Crave and Regal
and their black Quinn ink, rubbing my face into
bakeries and florists, the sweat of city buses,

I find another row of jackets where no row could be,
and walk onwards into leather and denim,
limited edition LPs, Lynn or Suzie pouting from empty
Tennant's lager tins, drawing me further into blazers,
football boots and Tupperware lunches,
until eventually, I walk onto Killynether.

At such times I curse my limited imagination.
But then I notice the colour of the grass,
its wet hair hum, and the underworld of tree trunks
and bluebells, the '99' clouds kiss-curling
from Comber to Croob, the peninsula's finger,
and its dawns on me I never knew the names

of ladies' smock or orange tips, the meadow
browns and ringlets; I never walked among
the celandine, silverweed, wood sage and clover;
never listened to the stonechats and linnets,
the stocking creepers fluttering over green-winged
orchids, twayblades, samphire or elder;

I never caught my shirt on a blazing hedge's
billhooks, by the blackthorn and dogwood,
gliding the breeze with the turnstones and terns,
hawking drumlins and pladdies, following wagtails
and warblers towards Jackdaw Island,
or Darragh Island by Ringhaddy Sound;

I never savoured the wave splash and salt spray,
the sandhoppers feeding on the strandline;
the horse mussels, bulrushes and lugworm casts,
shelducks, oystercatchers, widgeon and snipe
preying on the knotted wrack and eel-grass;
I was never entangled in dense forests of kelp;

I was never dragged beneath the surface
by velvet swimming crabs, to submarine
sand dunes with star pokers and dog cockles
or burrowing brittlestars; I never swam with thornback
rays or nurse hounds to the currents of the Narrows,
coming to rest with anemones and coral.

It's been years since I walked through Killynether.
When I wake I wonder if I've been there ever.
Sometime I must, before I flick the screen
and set about my business, or pick up the telephone,
wander over to the big lacquered wardrobe and open
negotiations with the stranger in the mirror.

YOU'LL NEVER WALK ALONE

She's dead set against the dead hand
of Belfast's walls guarding jinkered
cul-de-sacs, siderows, bottled sloganlands,

and the multinational malls' slicker
demarcations, their Xanadu of brands
entwining mind and income. Yet these replicas
atone for the brouhaha'd blare of the zones
she walks among, the bricked-in vigil of her home,

where they axed and hacked bark-stripped trees
and razed grass clearings, piled varnish-caked
crates and oil-slick tyres to a fire and stoned
dark-skinned refugees, broke Bacardi-Breezer
empties off kerbstones, paint-bombed windows,
raised their spray cans to new tenements,
built-up cans and butts like battlements
outside her door, and dreamed of burning green,
white and orange to ribbons that would rave
and rip through the dawn's zit of orange.

She walks by Little Britain merchandise,
made in China, and waits like a leper
in the darkened corridor of a debt advice
counsel room, listening to gangsta rappers
rapping that days slip by like grains of rice,
so she should shake her booty; that she is tapered
by time; that she should shed another skin;
that some days trampoline, flipping you outside-in.

'Such was the day'—I later heard her say,
soused in gin or doused with fontal waters
fallen from the apple-sliced, orange-peeling sky,

her shadow flaked as she wrangled for just
words—'such was the day, not when guerrillas
ate the protestors' livers before a village
crowd for opposing oil drills on TV;
nor when the bright lights flared over Baghdad's
orange, rose and *Tomb Raider* blue targets
trained by oil wells firing a welcome, or adieu;

nor when the dawn green ocean's heart attack
churned coastlines into troughs of corpse-stew;
when the earthquake turned tenements to smokestacks;
but the day I broke down and bawled myself blue
by my front door's graffiti, falling on the cracked,
coloured kerb with every bill overdue,
wishing the ground would gobble me whole, and
a neighbour asked if I needed a hand.'

BOB THE BUILDER IS A DICKHEAD

Some night when you're lost in a nest of narrow lanes
and you've forgotten where you're from, where you're going, again,

you'll think back and thank me for when you were three
and I threw out all your Bob the Builder DVDs.

I'm telling you now—Scoop, Dizzy, Lofty,
Muck and Rolly will make you soft and we

can't have you thinking you can fix it
every time the fan is hit with flying horseshit.

They want you to believe you should work for the team,
sacrifice yourself to a starched-collar dream,

but here's your choice: be shat upon or look out for No. 1;
either kick against the pricks, or else become one.

Balamory's full of Torys! Silence the Fat Controller
imposing his order on the island of Sodor!

But don't go bawling, this isn't Doomsday,
it's simply better things are spelled out this way.

For example, sex.
Pick up what you can at the local multiplex,

for soon your sanity will rely on
how well you placate your wee pyjama python.

Soon you'll do anything for your love's furry mouse,
so take her to Paris, or your favourite curry house

and buy her a lamb balti with a Cobra or Tiger,
rub her happy thigh as you sit down beside her,

but fastforward the scene by a couple of years
and you'll have nothing but Yesterday between your ears.

She'll have left you hopped-up, gormless, parched,
just one more wrinkle on the arse.

You'll want to whisk back on a magical broom
to that mystic split-second of your fusion in the womb:

to fly through celestial chaos, that cosmic hootenanny,
and find the divine factory where they sort out pricks from fannies.

There, you'll see the management office in order to destroy
the Goddess of Creation—who'll be announcing over the tannoy

with flat-packed officiousness:
'Welcome, customers! On entering consciousness,

please proceed directly to an impasse and fill
out a complaint form.' For this is Mission Impossible:

think positive, think negative—whatever you reckon,
your thoughts will self-destruct in fifteen seconds.

You'll end up on your knees seeking Holy Communion,
a taxpaying citizen of a multinational union.

Your American landlord will swing by in his Lexus,
take all your money, then fuck off back to Texas.

You might move from place to place, a mind-boggled rover,
or stay in Belfast where, although the war is over,

the Party of Bollocks and the Party of Balls
are locked in battle for the City Hall.

Even if you roam, you'll find it difficult
to avoid starvation and its twin, the cult

of profit backed by death planes firing vanity,
variable rates, trigger-fingered inanity.

But, of course, I might be wrong. Perhaps a constant
path exists for the fearless itinerant

to tread where, on the threshold of heaven,
the figures on the street become the figures of heaven

and our ears will alloy the preposterous babble.
One thing's for sure, every step will be a gamble.

Will it be paper, scissors, or stone?
Take another throw, son, of the devil's bones.

CARNIVAL

Black buffed leather-tongued brogues with oat-
meal socks and khaki Y-fronts, pleated slacks,
pert navy and gold striped double-windsored tie
on a twill non-iron white hassle-free shirt,

stiff blazer, wool felt bowler, dead white
gloves and orange sash with silver tassels,
marching onward, left, right, elbows tight
to Lambegs, banners, fifes, rows of waving
wives, marching onward, in formation, marching
on a Judas nation by the Queen's highway,
the town's High Street, roundabouts where forked
roads meet and never yield, marching to the field
of battle, field of peace, field patrolled by plain-
clothed police; field of Jesus, field of hope, field
of Bush and Fuck the Pope; marching onward into
heaven to scourge its halls of unwashed brethren;
then a blue bus home, content with your labours,
to watch *Countdown* and your favourite, *Neighbours*.

MORNING EMERGES OUT OF MUSIC

We dip, drop and dovetail in a cabaret
with crushed daiquiris and spellbound
maracas clippety-clapping the way
words click together and channel their sound
to a gorge-drop, a doorway, the sky-top's
blue veil. But then alarm bells ring, the music stops,
and I wake to a fade-out, an aftersound
of bebblers behind a curtain of air
that I chase through, my head dancing around
after rhythms without meaning, without care.

DRIVING HOME

I saw it coming, as I zipped and vroomed
headward from Coleraine to Belfast
under phone masts and sycamores
arching the flat road's tunnel through
hayfields, sun-gilt and harvests, my red
car careening in a fifth gear of freedom
past other cars' carbon fart trails,
cloudsmoked brushstrokes over scumbled
green horizons, every driver shooting
the bluetooth breeze with front windows
rolled to share their iPods' perfect playlists.

I saw it coming, as I left behind
the office and to-do lists; my boss, my other
boss, the other one again; that one's manager;
high priority email and enlarge your man-
hood spam; battery chicken, leathered ham pie;
visions of efficiency and a potted peace
lily that I'll have to water next time;
workmates eroticizing over calling it quits;
workmates swearing their colleagues are drooped shits;
squirly-whirlies on paper; the toilet floor *Star*;
a prissy car-park barrier blocking the car.

I saw it coming, loopy-go-lucky
muff-eared tongue-wagging happy-
as-sunlight mutt with scutched fawn coat:
a hop-skip-tittuping half-labrador

in a swagger chasing its own moist snout
filled with wonder, careening from sidepath
to roadway in a slavered rabbit dream,
leaving me two seconds to size up
I couldn't brake because the pimped-up
Micra up my ass was too near, too fast—
Dumph! It tail-chased death throes in the wing-
mirror spinning mad and bad-moon howling

out of sight. I'd no end of time to stop
but never did as the Micra overtook me,
for I might have had to carry that hyper-
ventilating half-corpse or matted carcass
with fleas and nothing in its eyes
up some farmyard lane to a child or sour
culchie into *Deliverance* and, anyway,
I wanted to get home to eat and channel-
surf for something decent or close my eyes
and drown in my sofa, so I hammered
headward down that road of sun and hay.

I va-va-voomed but the dog kept spinning
although left long behind, whirligigging
in a rear view of my mind so I couldn't
avert my eyes from that spinning jenny
death-dervish below the sky churning
buttermilk, lobster, apricot and kale.
The flat road lined with moonwort demanded
I turn back—but then I'd have to confess
I'd gone on for thirteen miles under pricked pines
hounding me, making me want to shunt

up to race-speed and take-off past the police
lurched with speed guns behind the '30' sign.

I might have pulled over and left
my car's front doors flung openwide —
a rickety carrier abandoned by picnic
tables in a litterblown parking bay
awaiting its lost passengers' return —
and hurled myself over the hedge to roam
google-eyed through deergrass and junipers
under a vanilla-rippled sky of crab shell,
tarragon and kelp to find a runnel
fleeced with bittercress and agrimony
where I'd lie and let the water-pepper
or salt-grass finger through me.

As I lay by the leak and lint of that runnel,
blaeberries and zigzag clover riddling
through me under puma-skinned skies,
I might have looked over the mantilla
of sheaves, stooks and stubble strewn across
that landscape of labrador downs,
or rolled beneath a yew to catch its leaves
contrailed by cream-slathered clouds
over the earth turning slowly around;
I might have lain and let flitter-fluttered birds
build their hay-nests in my eye-bowls
by the gash of that distant carriageway.

I might have drifted off, crossed over lanes
to collide in a slipstream of coming

and going, never here nor there but up
in the air, chasing homeward where to-do
lists are lurking, waiting for night to flip
my fried mind over until morning's
automatic return to the car and journey
back to that withered fantail of online
satellite navigation and in-car 3D
lapdance simulation, along those pointillist
phone masts and sycamores still arching
the road's bore through sun-gilt and harvest.

When I finally steered and veered the bend
into Belfast and turned into my street
I could have killed for a takeaway
but it was my turn to take the boy's
fire engine, fluffy dog and laser gun
to bed where we lay below his globed atlas lamp,
self-timed to fade, rotating projected
continents on the borderlined walls'
night-blue planetarium, where we read
until drift-off into nothing, unmoored
from the axled turn and low-watt embers
of the earth's spinning top left long behind.

A BLUEPRINT FOR SURVIVAL

I don't know you, you don't know me,
but if we want to carry on we need

to make like mountaineers who tie themselves
together to survive their clunt and grapple
up jagged peaks that shoot through clouds
into the shocked and haloed air.

If the weakest slows, the strongest grows
responsible, much like when you were born:
hot and bothered, you heard bad bongos
and withdrew your raw body from the verge;
so they took up the slack as you dandled
at the wrong end of your string, puffing
and wedging and pulling you back
to teeter and totter on this edge.

LAGAN WEIR

The way things are going
           there'll be no quick fix, no turning
back the way that flock of starlings
           skirls back on itself, then swerves forward,
swabbing and scrawling the shell-pink
           buffed sky, while I stand in two minds
on this scuffed bridge leaning over
           the fudged river that slooshes its dark way
to open harbours and the glistering sea.

Like flak from fire, a blizzard of evacuees,
           that hula-hooping sky-swarm of starlings

swoops and loops the dog-rose sky,
        while any way I look the writing's
on the wall. I watch the hurly-burlyed,
        humdrummed traffic belch to a stop,
fugging, clacking, charring the clotted air,
        making it clear things are going to get
a whole lot worse before they get better.

That flickered, fluttered hurry-scurry
        of starlings sweeps left, then swishes right
through the violet sky while I huddle
        and huff, with a dove in one ear saying
look the other way, a hawk in the other
        braying self-righteous fury. It's hard
not to turn back to a time when one look
        at you and I knew things were going to get
a whole lot better before they'd get worse.

That hue and cry, those hurricanes
        of starlings swoosh and swirl their fractals
over towers, hotels, hospitals, flyovers,
catamarans, city-dwellers, passers-through,
        who might as well take a leap and try following
after that scatter-wheeling circus of shadows
        as slowly turn and make their dark way
homeward, never slowing, not knowing
        the way things are going.

LEONTIA FLYNN

[B. 1974]

EEPS

So I'm wondering was my father a prophet
when — as often — one of his little wires came loose
in the light fitting with the brass surround on our white porch wall

and he hauled us — we were seven — in crocodile formation
to the scrubbed white porch with the faulty light fitting,
where planted his thumb — like a crocodile-clip — to the brass

— and the base, like a touch-paper, crackled — as wild eeps and ozone
went flocking — not minding the gap — to the end of the line
which might now be this scattered, flickering parish

the quick jab on the X key; this brief thrill on the hand . . .

THE MIRACLE OF F6/18

Walking with him was like walking somehow in shadow.
The sun went out of her way to keep us in the dark.
Once, I was told, as he was entering a friend's house
the lightbulbs — even the fridge's — exploded in splintering hail.
And it should have been easy had he not broken every rule
like when I awoke — I had laboured, his little handmaiden! —
to find him by the bedside: his face, in a kind of cloud,

was the face of a stranger; and so I dozed again,
and so I woke—to find him, in negative, lying
—like the Turin Shroud—on this white sheet of my memory.

WITHOUT ME

Without me I have been without you I
have lost my bearings I have lost the key
on the heart-shaped fob—the talisman you gave me.

July the tenth, 1999
and from the sky comes the Great King of Terror.

But Sylvia gulps a paroxetine with soda
and snaps—with her teeth—the magic thread
whose breadth is a hair-trigger.

So, Sylvia, go on, snap the magic thread
between feeling—feeling everything, feeling nothing.

MY DREAM MENTOR

My dream mentor sits in his room overlooking the city.
He can see the far swell of the Pentlands, the folk milling below

hapless as maggots. So we sit there in silence
like a couple of kids in the bath, till he says:

If you can't be a prodigy, there's no point trying.
Don't fall for the one about the drunk, queuing in Woolworths,
who tells you his Gaelic opus was seized by the state.
If you can fashion something with a file in it for the academics
to hone their malicious nails on—you're minted.
And another thing, don't write about anything
                                        you can point at.

SNOW

When the academic year of a millennium
winds itself, wheezily, into the siding
where will you find me?

Running like a girl
for the love of a fast-track train
back to the fish-smelling ferry terminal.
The sea raises a glass—rosé—to the sky at Troon.

But something is blocking the line.
It's leaves perhaps—or that other obstinate cliché:
the wrong kind of snow.

NOCTURNE

Trying to figure that *je ne sais quoi* a poem takes to get published:
a clerical temp, capitalising on the caesura
in his working day—sweet little night enjambing
from the blue scraps of his evening.

He is sat with a pointed stick by this sheet of fly-paper,
the words not coming.
(Though his lines are coming down with feminine endings.)

My tongue cleaves to my mouth O Lord, The Words not coming
he writes, The Words not . . . Wha?
       Whaddya mean already written? What?
Louis? Louis who?

WITHOUT ME

Once, in the hiatus of a difficult July,
down Eskra's lorryless roads from sweet fuck all,
we were flinging—such young sophisticates—like a giant frisbee
this plastic lid of an old rat-poison bin.

We were flinging it from you to me, me to you, you to me;
me-you, you-me, me-you, you back again.

And you would have sworn that its flat arc was a pendulum,
compassing Tyrone's prosy horizon.

And I would have sworn that our throw and catch had such momentum
that its rhythm might survive, somehow, without me.

A PAUSE

There is a pause in the middle of conversation
during which time we absently get to our feet
put on our coats, our terrible secondhand hats,
and walk for fifteen minutes to the demolished all-night shop.

When we return, what stops us isn't the locks
—which won't have changed, like the ancient décor:
(the 'chesterfield suite', the oiled patch, like an antimacassar
where you rested your head, that flock

wallpaper)—but the sight of our small brick
garden, thick with dandelion clocks.

PERL POEM

Surrounded by bric-a-brac—mugs of stale coffee and old
    manuals—Lawrence works at his desk.
His computer screen burns like a Cyclops' eye. He is
    writing programs
for drinks companies in Dublin—helping keep Ireland,
    North and South, awash with hooch.

```
while ( <FHND> ) { s/\x0a/\x0d\x0a/g; push (
   @m_arr, Hio:parse ( $_ ) ) ; } ..., he writes,
for ( $i; $i < @m_arr; $i++ ) { print FHND
   $m_arr[ $i ] ; } .
```

Programming language, he says, is no dry, fussy
    abstraction. There's tremendous wit
in its usage: the elegance of Perl—Edwin Morgin's 'great,
    final ease of creation'
in tuning the lines most perfectly to their function. It's
    not science fiction.
It's not like: *If we can just hack into the mainframe of the computer*
we should be able to upload the virus on to the mothership.

And it's not like poetry; it doesn't log out or go off into
    the ether freighted only with itself;
it walks a network of roads, getting dust on its feet and
    saying hi to people—

```
sub cZap { my $sig = shift; &cleanup; die
   "Recd: SIG$sig\n"; } $SIG{ INT} = \&cZap; —
```

It doesn't hover over the country—like poetry does—
    like a special effect.

APRIL, 7 P.M.

Where our phone wires meet
over those terraces — look
the sky is still blue!

HOLLAND

I

The rattling noise from the heater in the daffodil shed
has assumed the rhythm of the production line
where now you continually pack and unpack yourself;
it's insane that in the longest part of the night
there's a moment to think of Larkin's 'incessant recital'
in *If, my Darling* — was *this* what he meant?
This world unpicked by 'meaning and meaning's rebuttal'?

II

The Dutch doctor with the brunette handlebar moustache
smiles sadly as he prescribes Oxazypam
(are these *cow* tranquillisers?), giving a little shrug
at his own proposal to 'avoid these with alcohol',
then taking your grime-stained urchin's hand, he adds
'If I live in Belfast, I also perhaps feel bad.'
Now even your *neuroses* are unoriginal.

THESE DAYS

for Catherine Donnelly

These days, it seems, I am winding my clock an hour forward
with every second weekend, and the leaves on my Marc Chagall calendar
flip as though they are caught in some covert draught.
These days I haven't time for people on television or aeroplanes
who say 'momentarily' meaning 'in just one moment'.

These days—these days which are fairly unremarkable—
light falls, outside of my window, on the red brick planes
where the trees are coming into leaf. These are the days
of correcting the grammar on library-desk graffiti,
the cheap, unmistakeable thrill of breaking a copyright law.

But these days, like Cleopatra's Antony, I fancy bestriding the ocean;
these days I am serious. These days I'm bowled over
hearing myself say *ten years ago this . . . ten years ago such-and-such*
like the man left standing, his house falling wall by wall,
in that black-and-white flick blurring headlong into colour.

NICK LAIRD

[B. 1975]

REMAINDERMEN

Because what I liked about them best
was their ability to thole,
that weathered silence and reluctance,
fornenst the whole damn lot.

They've lived alone for years of course,
and watched their cemeteries filling up
like car parks on a Saturday,
their young grow fat for export.

There are others who know what it is
to lose, to hold ideas of north
so singularly brutal that the world
might be ice-bound for good.

Someone has almost transcribed
the last fifty years of our speech,
and has not once had the chance
to employ the word *sorry*

or press the shift to make the mark
that indicates the putting of a question.
The arch was put up wrong this Spring
outside my father's office.

When you enter it states
Safe Home Brethren,
and upon leaving the place
Welcome Here.

DONE

We've come to bag the evidence.
This might be the scene of a murder.
Dustsheets and silence and blame.

The flat empties its stomach into the hall.
We have given back letters and eaten our words.
You wrote off the Volvo. I gave you verrucas.

And like the window of a jeweller's after closing
the shelves in the study offer up nothing.
I slowly take the steps down one by one,

and for the first time maybe,
notice the chaos, the smouldering traffic,
the litter, bystanders, what have you

THE LAST SATURDAY IN ULSTER

Behind her radiator
the leather purse is caring
for the old denominations:
liverspots of giant pennies,
fifty pences thick as lenses.

A Pentecostal home outside Armagh:
antimacassars, oxygen masks,
Martha glancing towards the screen
as if checking delay and departure.

An Orange march in Antrim
will see me late arriving:
and standing out at Aldergrove
an English girl might well believe
that time is how you spend your love.

Undriven cattle graze the long acre.
Pheasants fidget and flit between townlands.
The coins were warm as new eggs
in the nest of her priestly-cool hands.

A GUIDE TO MODERN WARSAW

The striplights
that illuminate the working late

have made my block
a latticework of boxed-up stars and dark:

it looks like the negative and inverse
of a letter, black-lined by the censor,

attempting to explain through injured syntax
and discussion mainly on the weather

that what will come for us
is air-conditioned, plushly fast,

and moves so smoothly on its tracks
that we'll stay crumpled, dead to the world,

when it pauses near the skyscraper,
the first ever built in Warsaw,

which demonstrates its brand awareness
on the site of the Great Synagogue

with a massive Sony mark
countersigned at pavement level

by twenty-six graffiti tags, eleven
printed pamphlets advertising prostitutes

or lessons in the martial arts,
and nine pleas for missing dogs.

EVERYMAN

Thou comest when I had thee least in mind.

The hellmouth, to begin with,
three fathom of cord and a windlass,
a link to fire the tinder.

An earthquake: barrel for the same —
we gathered stones the size of fists each time
and rolled them round in it.

Also, a pageant, that is to say,
a house of wainscot,
painted and builded on a cart with four wheels.

A square top to set over said house.
One griffon, gilt,
with a fane to set on said top.

■

Heaven, England, and Hell:
the three worlds we painted as backdrops,
when we left Norwich,

that winter so cold
the rivers slowed to silver roads,
and the oxen thinned to bone.

A rib coloured red.
Two coats and a pair hosen for Eve, stained.
A coat and hosen for Adam, stained.

A face and hair for the Father.
Two hairs for Adam and Eve.
Two pair of gallows. Four scourges. A pillar.

■

The Year of Our Lord I started the record
for the Coventry Drapers Company
was fifteen hundred and thirty-eight.

Autumns, we'd burn leaves
in cauldrons. In summer
straw would serve, or bark.

If the fire didn't take,
a monstrous Dragon's Mouth
would counterfeit the way below.

Come the new moon from the velvet bag
I drew one shilling five for Thomas and wife,
and six pence for Luke Brown, playing God.

■

The Castle of Perseverance.
Abraham and Isaac.
The Judgement. Noah's Flood.

Each mechanical effect
brought bleats of sudden wonder,
the windlass to lower, the barrel to roll,

the link to set light to the tinder,
although no sound was quite the sound—
that catch of breath caught by the crowd—

when Knowledge, Beauty, Good Deeds,
would take their exit left
and from the right, wordlessly, came Death.

LIGHT POLLUTION

You're the patron saint of elsewhere,
jet-lagged and drinking apple juice,
eyeing, from the sixth-floor window,
a kidney-shaped swimming pool
the very shade of Hockney blue.

I know the left-hand view of life,
I think, and it's as if I have, of late,
forgotten something in the night—
I wake alone and freezing,
still keeping to my side.

Each evening tidal night rolls in
and the atmosphere is granted
a depth of field by satellites,
the hammock moon, aircraft
sinking into Heathrow.

Above the light pollution,
among the drift of stars tonight
there might be other traffic—
migrations of heron and crane,
their spectral skeins convergent

symbols, arrows, weather systems,
white flotillas bearing steadily
towards their summer feeding.
A million flapping sheets!
Who knows how they know?

The aids to navigation might be
memory and landmarks,
or the brightest constellations.
Perhaps some iron in the blood
detects magnetic north.

I wish one carried you some token,
some Post-it note or ticket,
some particular to document
this instant of self-pity—
His Orphic Loneliness, with Dog.

Advances? None miraculous,
though the deadness of the house
will mean your coming home
may seem an anticlimax
somehow, and a trespass.

LEAVING THE SCENE OF AN ACCIDENT

Stalagmites of bird-lime
under traffic lights and statues,
the unrumbled railway bridges.

Books obsolesce in lockers.
A stork in April makes a nest
in the second reactor's tower.

Like a deep foundation crack,
a single strand of ivy climbs
the gable of the courthouse.

■

In the eastern suburbs deer appear.
Brushed by waist-high silver steppe grass
and the lighter strokes of barley stalks,

elegant as one might half-expect
the grazing self to be, except her grace
is one complicit in departure.

At the snap and flutter of a shopping bag
snagged in branches, she will break,
and overtake her shadow in the café window.

■

A wolf, one afternoon in August,
sauntered through the old town square.
By dawn a score were there,

parading past the main post office,
splashing in the People's Fountain,
drinking from it, basking, snarling.

After the storms of autumn pass
black sturgeon ripple, in their turn,
the perfectly circular cooling ponds.

APPRAISAL

Features? Embarrassed by their faeces,
omnivorous and sad, awkward beasts
dependent on their tightly metred breath

to keep on feeding, sleeping, breeding.
Oddly they prohibit eating certain species,
like guinea pigs or golden lemurs,

any kind of creatures who can crease
their hairless faces into wrinkles: amusement,
is it, or the purest, dumbest recognition.

They laugh, yes, and snort, and stifle sneezes,
and though they sport the same thin fleeces
in the southern droughts and northern freezes,

so instinctively aggressive is the genus
that they herd in such a way to leave the weakest
prey to what might find it easiest to eat.

Still, wide-eyed in the darkness they fear it.
Part-rational, part-mammal, part-bastard,
yanked along perpetually on leashes by their genes.

Their minds may shine with language, fine,
but what good's that? Words are just pieces like they are,
poor fuckers, who sit on their own in the small hours,

warming a grievance, talking aloud, articulating
tiny myths of struggle and deliverance.
I think they're appealing. I don't mean as in pleasing.

USE OF SPIES

Upright and sleepless,
having watched three bad movies,
I am flying across the ocean to see you.

I am a warrior and nothing will stop me,
although in the event both passport control
and a stoned cabbie from Haiti will give it a go,

but I meant to mention something else.

Just before dinner I woke in mid-air,
opened the shutter and saw the sun rising.
Light swung over the clouds like a boom.

The way it broke continually from blue
to white was beautiful, like some fabled
giant wave that people travel years to catch.

I thought I'll have to try and tell you that.

THE HALL OF MEDIUM HARMONY

In lieu of a Gideon Bible
      the bedside table drawer
has a *Lonely Planet Guide to China*
      and a year-old *Autotrader.*

You skim through the soft-tops, the imports,
      the salvage & breakers,
then pick up the book. Over there
      they are eight hours ahead

so it must be approximately dawn
      in the Forbidden City,
where something might evade the guides
      already at the entrance,

might glide right past the lion-dogs
      on guard, asleep in bronze,
might fire the dew on the golden tiles,
      ignite each phoenix on its ridge.

Light. Nine-thousand nine-hundred
      and ninety-nine rooms
begin to warm under its palm.
      Here, in the book, is a diagram.

There is the Hall of Union and Peace.
      The Hall of Medium Harmony.
The Meridian Gate. The Imperial Library.
      The inner golden bridges.

You fidget. You are, you admit, one of
      the earth's more nervous passengers.
But it's different, this, a reasonable space.
      In the palace of an afternoon

a child-king hiding in the curtain
      listening. For a second apart
from the turn of the thing, for a second
      forgetting the narrative's forfeit—

how nothing can outlast its loss,
      that solace is found, if at all,
in the silence that follows each footstep
      let fall on the black lacquer floor

of the now, of the here, where you are,
      in the sunlight, blinking, abroad.

BIOGRAPHIES

CHRIS AGEE was born in 1956 and grew up in Massachusetts, Rhode Island and New York. He attended Harvard University and since 1979 has lived in Ireland. He is the author of three collections of poems, *In the New Hampshire Woods* (The Dedalus Press, 1992), *First Light* (The Dedalus Press, 2003) and *Next to Nothing* (Salt, 2008), as well as the editor of *Scar on the Stone: Contemporary Poetry from Bosnia* (Bloodaxe Books, 1998) and *Unfinished Ireland: Essays on Hubert Butler* (Irish Pages, 2003). He reviews regularly for *The Irish Times* and is the Editor of *Irish Pages*, a journal of contemporary writing based at the Linen Hall Library, Belfast.

GARY ALLEN was born in Ballymena, Co Antrim in 1959. He worked and travelled widely in continental Europe, settling for a period in Holland. He is the author of three collections of poetry, *Languages* (Flambard, 2002), *Exile* (Black Mountain Press, 2004) and *North of Nowhere* (Lagan Press, 2006). He continues to live in Ballymena, where he writes full-time.

JEAN BLEAKNEY was born in Newry, Co Down in 1956 and attended Queen's University Belfast. She has published two collections of poems, *The Ripple Tank Experiment* (Lagan Press, 1999) and *The Poet's Ivy* (Lagan Press, 2003). Formerly a biochemist, she now works in a garden centre in Belfast.

MOYRA DONALDSON was born in Newtownards in 1956 and attended Queen's University Belfast. She is the author of three collections of poems, *Snakeskin Stilettos* (1998), *Beneath the Ice* (2001) and *The Horse's Nest* (2006), all from Lagan Press. She works as a social worker in Belfast.

LEONTIA FLYNN was born in 1973 in Belfast and attended Queen's University Belfast and University of Edinburgh. Her first collection, *These Days* (Cape), appeared in 2004. A second, *Drives*, is forthcoming. She is currently Research Fellow at the Seamus Heaney Centre for Poetry, Queen's University Belfast.

ALAN GILLIS was born in 1973 in Belfast and attended Queen's University Belfast. He is the author of two collections of poems, *Somebody, Somewhere* (The Gallery Press, 2004) and *Hawks and Doves* (The Gallery Press, 2007), as well as a critical study, *Irish Poetry of the 1930s* (Oxford University Press, 2005). He co-edited, with Aaron Kelly, *Critical Ireland: New Essays on Literature and Culture* (Four Courts Press, 2001). He lives in Edinburgh and teaches in the Department of English Literature, University of Edinburgh.

PAUL GRATTAN was born in Glasgow in 1971 and grew up in Scotland. He attended Strathclyde University before moving to Northern Ireland in 1995. His first collection of poems is *The End of Napoleon's Nose* (Edinburgh Review, 2002). He now lives in Belfast, where he works as a teacher.

MATT KIRKHAM was born in Luton, England, in 1966 and attended Cambridge University. He first came to Northern Ireland for a year in 1989 and moved to Belfast in 1995. His first collection of poems, *The Lost Museums* (Lagan Press), appeared in 2006. He lives on the Ards peninsula, near Belfast, and works as a teacher.

NICK LAIRD was born in 1975 in Cookstown, Co Tyrone, and attended Cambridge University. He lived for periods in Boston and Warsaw. He is the author of two collections of poems, *To a Fault* (Faber and Faber, 2005) and *On Purpose* (Faber and Faber, 2007), as well as a novel, *Utterly Monkey* (Fourth Estate, 2005). He now lives in Kilburn, London, where he writes full-time.

GEARÓID MAC LOCHLAINN was born in 1966, grew up in West Belfast, and attended Queen's University Belfast. His poetry collections are *Babylon Gaeligeoir* (An Clochán, 1997), *Na Scéalaithe* (Coiscéim, 1999), the bilingual *Sruth Teangacha/Stream of Tongues* (Cló Iar-Chonnachta, 2002), and *Rakish Paddy Blues* (Open House Festival, 2004). He was formerly a musician with the reggae band, Breág, and was Writer-in-Residence in the Irish Language at the University of Ulster and Queen's University Belfast from 2002 to 2005.

SINÉAD MORRISSEY was born in Portadown in 1972 and attended Trinity College, Dublin. She lived and worked for periods in Japan and New Zealand. She has published three collections of poems, *There Was Fire in Vancouver* (1996), *Between Here and There* (2002) and *The State of the Prisons* (2005), all from Carcanet Press. She is Lecturer in Creative Writing at the Seamus Heaney Centre for Poetry, Queen's University Belfast.

CATHAL Ó SEARCAIGH was born in 1956 and raised in Meenala, near Gortahork, an Irish-speaking district in Co Donegal. He was Writer-in-Residence in the Irish Language at the University of Ulster and Queen's University Belfast for three years in the early nineties, and continues to be a regular visitor to Northern Ireland, where he is an important presence for the Irish-speaking community. His poetry collections are *Súile Shuibhne* (Coiscéim, 1983), *Suibhne* (Coiscéim, 1987), the bilingual *An Bealach 'na Bhaile/ Homecoming* (Cló Iar-Chonnachta, 1993), *Ag Tnúth Leis an tSolas* (Cló Iar-Chonnachta, 1993), *Na Buachaillí Bána* (Cló Iar-Chonnachta, 1996), and the selected *Out in the Open* (Cló Iar-Chonnachta, 2000). He is also the author of a work of non-fiction, *Séal Neipeal* (Cló Iar-Chonnachta, 2004) and several plays in Irish. A selection of English translations of his poetry, *By the Hearth at Mín a' Leá* (Arc), appeared in 2005. He continues to live in Meenala.

FRANK SEWELL was born in 1968 in Nottingham, England, and grew up in Belfast. He attended Queen's University Belfast and the University of Ulster at Coleraine. His first joint collection of poems, with Francis O'Hare, was *Outside the Walls* (An Clochán, 1997), and his second *How the Light Gets In* (Cranagh Press, 1999). He is the author of a monograph, *Modern Irish Poetry: A New Alhambra* (Oxford University Press, 2000) and co-translator from the Japanese, with Mitsuko Ohno, of *Beyond the Hedge: New and Selected Poems*, by Mutsuo Takahashi (The Dedalus Press, 2006). He has also translated widely from Russian and Irish-language poetry. He currently teaches in the English Department at the University of Ulster, Coleraine.

DAMIAN SMYTH was born in Downpatrick, Co Down, in 1962. He is the author of two collections of poems, *Downpatrick Races* (Lagan Press, 2000) and *The Down Recorder* (Lagan Press, 2004), as well as a play, *Soldiers of the Queen* (Lagan Press, 2002). He is the Literature Officer of the Arts Council of Northern Ireland and lives in Belfast.

ANDY WHITE was born in Belfast in 1962 and attended Cambridge University. He has been writing songs and recording music since 1986, producing 12 albums to date and touring extensively. His first collection of poems, *The Music of What Happens* (Lagan Press), appeared in 1998. He currently lives in Melbourne, Australia.

PERMISSIONS

Grateful acknowledgment is made to: Gary Allen for permission to reprint seven poems from *Languages* (2002) and *Exile* (2004). Cape Poetry for permission to reprint twelve poems by Leontia Flynn from *These Days* (2004). Cape Poetry for permission to reprint three poems by Michael Longley from *Collected Poems* (2006). Carcanet Press Limited for permission to reprint twelve poems by Sinéad Morrissey from *There Was Fire in Vancouver* (1996), *Between Here and There* (2002) and *The State of the Prisons* (2005). Cló Iar-Chonnachta for permission to reprint nine poems by Cathal Ó Searcaigh from *An Bealach 'na Bhaile/Homecoming* (1993) and *Out in the Open* (2000). W. W. Norton and Company for permission to reprint ten poems by Nick Laird from *To a Fault* (2005) and *On Purpose* (2007). Farrar, Straus and Giroux for permission to reprint four poems by Paul Muldoon from *New and Selected Poems: 1968–1994*. Farrar, Straus and Giroux for permission to reprint three poems by Seamus Heaney from *Opened Ground: Selected Poems, 1966–1996*. Frank Sewell for permission to reprint two poems from *Outside the Walls* (1997). Paul Grattan for permission to reprint eight poems from *The End of Napoleon's Nose* (2002). Lagan Press for permission to reprint fourteen poems by Andy White from *The Music of What Happens* (1998). Lagan Press for permission to reprint eleven poems by Damian Smyth from *Downpatrick Races* (2000) and *The Down Recorder* (2004). Lagan Press for permission to reprint four poems by Gary Allen from *North of Nowhere* (2006). Lagan Press for permission to reprint ten poems by Jean Bleakney from *The Ripple Tank Experiment* (1999) and *The Poet's Ivy* (2003). Lagan Press for permission to reprint fourteen poems by Matt Kirkham from *The Lost Museums* (2006). Lagan Press for permission to reprint eight poems by Moyra Donaldson from *Snakeskin Stilettos* (1998) and *Beneath the Ice* (2001). Gearóid Mac Lochlainn for permission to reprint ten poems from *Sruth Teangacha/Stream of Tongues* (2002). Salt Publishing for permission to reprint three poems by Chris Agee from *Next to Nothing* (2008). The Dedalus Press for permission to reprint seven poems by Chris Agee from *In the New Hampshire Woods* (1992) and *First Light* (2003). The Gallery Press for permission to reprint fourteen poems by Alan Gillis from *Somebody, Somewhere* (2004) and *Hawks and Doves* (2007). The Gallery Press for permission to reprint three poems by Derek Mahon from *Collected Poems* (1999). The Gallery Press for permission to reprint two poems by Medbh McGuckian from *The Flower Master and Other Poems* (1993).

Every effort has been made to trace and contact copyright holders before publication. If notified, the publisher will rectify any errors or omissions at the earliest opportunity.